PRAISE FOR "GOOD TO GO'

I love this book, which is beautifully written and full of interesting stories, poetry, and wisdom. While there is something in us that is afraid of death, there is also something in us that is not afraid of death. *Good to Go* helps us to recognize and trust whatever it is in ourselves that is not afraid, so we can face whatever comes with open and peaceful hearts.

— MICHAEL KEARNEY, M.D., Palliative Care & Hospice Doctor, Cottage Health, Author of *A Place of Healing: Working with Nature and Soul at the End of Life* and *The Nest in the Stream*

Dr. Horton is an exceptional physician who has spent a lifetime attempting to facilitate communications between patients and their doctors and patients and their families. He has written a brilliant book summarizing his life's experience regarding preparations for dying well. This book is a must for anyone who has loved ones who may be grappling with this issue. It is a masterpiece.

— PHILIP WILLIAM GOLD, M.D., Library of Congress Council of Scholars, former Investigator in the Intramural Research Program of the NIMH, Author of *Breaking Through Depression*

In an ideal world, *Good to Go* would be required reading in every medical school the world over, enabling the next generation of doctors to live their Hippocratic oath with much more wisdom, tenderness and consciousness. But the audience for the book goes far beyond the medical world. It's for everyone— written in a way that goes down easy.

— MITCH DITKOFF, Author of *Unspoken Word: Love Longing & Letting Go* and *Storytelling for the Revolution*

Good to Go is full of valuable lessons for a better life learned from those in their last chapter. A powerful guide to becoming unafraid of death. — Susan Stiffelman, MFT, Author of *Parenting Without Power Struggles* and *Parenting with Presence*

Ultimately, the authors want readers to understand that in everybody is something that does not die and can be enjoyed until and perhaps through the very end. A gentle, well-considered guidebook for making peace with life's end.

— Kirkus Review

If you're not nervous about dying, then there is something wrong with you. What Dr. Horton has done with *Good to Go* is give you the information you need to not feel nervous. And he does it in an easily digestible format using five simple points that are very comforting.

— Barton Goldsmith, Ph.D., Author of *Emotional Fitness* book series, newspaper column, and blog.

In each relatable story, Dr Horton identifies fears about death we must overcome and the understandings we can, if we try and are properly supported, develop to help us achieve a more comfortable, safe, and reflected-upon death, one in which we may reconnect to our inner peace, joy, clarity, and even an elegant grace.

— Steven J. Danenberg, retired Head of School of The Pomfret School, The Country School, and The Williams School

This book is a simple yet profound source of gentle wisdom for all stages of life. *Good To Go* provides heartfelt examples that helps us in understanding the best way to approach this last process of our existence. Not only can we begin to recognize what this transition means, but this book also helps us to better support and show compassion for those who are approaching this most unique life event.

— Chris Corbett, Author of *The White Game* and *Nirvana Blues*

Good to Go is the ultimate user manual for conscious living, dying and caregiving from a doctor with 50 years of experience. The reader finds a treasure trove of stories that guide us through the wonderful possibilities and realities of our "last journey." I'm good to go, and this book is a gem!

— CYNTHIA FITZPATRICK, award-winning Filmmaker

At the heart of *Good to Go* is a message of love. I am deeply touched and profoundly grateful to John for sharing the invaluable lessons gleaned from his patients, his vast medical experience, and his diverse cultural encounters. *Good to Go* is truly a gift and essential reading for all, offering deep wisdom and solace to those navigating their own mortality or supporting loved ones through their final journey.

— LAUREN Z. SCHNEIDER, MFT, Psychotherapist, Speaker, Author of *Tarotpy: It's All in the Cards*

John Horton's new book is a treasury of stories that set the stage for one's last phase of life. Dr. Hortons teachings are offered amidst his intricately woven stories of those he has helped and attended to as patients and friends nearing the end of their lives. I strongly recommend this book to everyone wanting a new perspective on life and it's conclusion.

— TAMARA MEYERS, Educator, Author

I have known Dr. Horton's remarkable work and wisdom for over 50 years. So, it was with great pleasure when I read *Good to Go* with Sushila Wood, the latest extension of his unique knowledge and wisdom to the final chapter of all our lives.

— JAMES C. BALLENGER, M.D., former Director of the Institute of Psychiatry; the Center for Drug and Alcohol Programs at the Medical University of SC in Charleston, SC

Good to Go

Good to Go

Five Understandings to Navigate a Peaceful and Elegant Last Chapter of Life

John Horton, MD
Sushila Wood

New Insights Press

Editorial Direction and Editing: Rick Benzel Creative Services
Cover and Book Design: Susan Shankin & Associates
Published by New Insights Press, Los Angeles, CA
www.newinsightspress.com

ISBN: 979-8-9894926-0-2
Library of Congress Control Number: 2023923876
Printed in the United States of America

To waking up to the beauty of existence.
It is never too late.
~ John Horton, MD

For the awe of a human life.
~ Sushila Wood

When it comes to the end,
maybe we become sick of living,
but afraid of dying.

You can get to a good place.
These stories give understanding and
hope that each of us can find that path,
and be good to go.

Contents

Foreword

WHEN I FIRST WROTE *THE INNER GAME OF TENNIS,* I discovered the significant difference between our innate abilities and what we teach one another. The human body and human consciousness are essential for learning the important things in life, including playing a good game of tennis or golf.

When Dr. John Horton and I collaborated with our friend, Dr. Edd Hanzelik, to write *The Inner Game of Stress,* I realized that our health and wellbeing are also helped by innate resources as well as the science of medicine. I see that John has been able to appreciate this and utilize it in his work throughout the over fifty years of our wonderful friendship.

How interesting that in the very last hours of life, it is never too late to dwell in peace and inner contentment. This is what I find most valuable in reading the stories of Dr. John's fine book; it is never too late.

I like the title of this book, because I know that someday I too, as well as you readers, can be "good to go" when our time comes and that we can go in peace and at harmony within ourselves. This is a very hopeful message and can do much to allay the natural and prevalent fears of dying. If you want to go in peace, *Good to Go* defines the inner game to play before you die.

As with many people in my age group, the 80s, I am enchanted by very young children. I see the innate innocence, excitement and joy in their actions. Then in their quiet moments, I can see the tranquility and peacefulness of their hearts, so attractive. I know for sure that these qualities of existence are innate and seem to me perfect. I am hopeful that I will be able to dwell in my heart and the excitement of existence until my very last breaths. This would be the ultimate success of the *Inner Game.*

I take both courage and clarity from Dr. Horton's departed patients, as well as the profound understanding John has gained over many years talking with patients and letting go of his own fears. *Good to Go* sets a high standard to reach, but all the understandings are sketched out in these pages in simple terms—ones that I feel hopeful I can remember along the way—because the stories are interesting, relatable, and inspiring.

—Tim Gallwey, author of the *New York Times* bestselling *Inner Game* series of books.

Introduction

GEORGE BURNS THE AMERICAN HUMORIST HAD THIS to say about dying:

"Death has been around a long time but it has never gained in popularity."

There is a similar sentiment from the ancient epic Indian classic, the Mahabharata:

Of all things in life, what is most amazing?
That a man, seeing others die all around him,
never thinks he will die.

I almost died in the mountains of Basutoland, now called Lesotho, in the early spring of 1965. The experience literally changed everything in my life. It was not a dramatic near-death experience, no tunnel in front of me, no appearance of a being of light, but the result was life changing. The cause of this possible death was not dramatic either. I was just slowly freezing to death.

I was then a volunteer in a remote Southern African flying doctor service, having left Dartmouth College to find more meaning in my life. It was a good adventure and a rite of passage, living in remote villages accessible only by a single engine plane or by horse or on foot. Little food, no plumbing, thatched huts, flies everywhere, and wonderful kind people.

A few Lesotho men and I had been spent the day assembling a corrugated steel clinic hut some distance from the nearest village. The night had come quickly and with no flashlights, we could not safely navigate the rocky narrow mountain trail to get back to the village. We made a fire and the men wrapped themselves in their blankets while I tried to sleep in my jeans and tee shirt. It had been quite hot during the day. Until that night close to death, life had been about my achievements — past, current, and those possible in the future. The next few days, I became focused on my feeling of inner peace and the fact that in those simple mountain villages, people were content. Inner contentment and personal peace were new possibilities for me. This feeling of a deep peace for no reason lasted only a few weeks, but it prepared me for future discoveries of the capacity of my heart — and every human heart — to feel a timeless peace.

It is never too late to know this peaceful foundation of our existence. It is fitting that we come into this life knowing this peace, and then when we are ripe to depart, we can rediscover this same peace again. Of course, the best is to know this peace every day and even every minute of our life. This is a possibility, though few achieve it.

In the years that followed, during my time at Duke Medical School in Durham, North Carolina and then my internship in pediatrics, medicine, and psychiatry at San Francisco General Hospital in California, I lost this peace and the goodness of my encounter with death. What replaced it was anxiety and fear about death, now as a doctor seeing people die in the hospital environment. Death seemed terrible and mostly traumatic to everyone. There was no medical training in those days to deal with death.

Since then, I have learned a great deal about death. This book contains the stories of the people who I have had the good fortune to meet and treat as they approached death and passed on. Their efforts and mine have allowed me to present to you five understandings" to make your own departure safe, comfortable, peaceful, and perhaps even elegant. Such a death involves a real understanding of the nature of your inner life as well as avoiding the bullets of unnecessary futile medicine, i.e., treatment that keeps you alive despite your having no quality of life.

These five understandings are necessary and sufficient for a death where you can be at peace with yourself and others. After all, both being born and dying are an expression of the mystery of human consciousness. Understanding our existence is based more on feeling than intellect. As the French philosopher Pascal said, "The heart has its reasons which reason does not know."

If you are fortunate enough to have some time towards the end of life to approach death consciously, this book can have value for you and those loved ones around you. Most of us would like to die quietly in our sleep without loss of physical or mental functioning — a quick, painless end without any prolonged medical care. Or perhaps a sudden accident or heart attack that doesn't cause any inconvenience. Good luck with that, as this type of death is not what most of us will encounter in our last phase of life.

There is goodness in a comfortable, safe, reflected-upon death just as there is in an uncomplicated birth. Both ends of life are part of the beauty of nature and the deep goodness of human consciousness. A laboring mother can make a commitment to allow herself the space and time. A mother can trust in her body to naturally produce the hormones required to tolerate the whole birthing experience. No matter how painful or how many hours, that trust can be solid. When the time comes for our exit, however, can we create equally favorable conditions needed to help us let go? It's not so physical in the end; it is more emotional and mental. Though it is a very different kind of effort than birthing, if we are caught in anxiety and worry, things can get stuck just like a mother's labor can stall if she does not feel safe.

In the end, perhaps we can only be *good to go* if we have the time and space to find a path where we can safely allow our body to let go. It is more a question of avoiding obstacles than of creating or doing anything. The child in the womb is connected to something wonderful. We too can be connected to that something wonderful as we let go of everything here. As our life winds down, many obligations and desires will be off our plate. When there is nothing left, we can see the plate for what it is — the gift of human consciousness. That is wonderful in itself.

It is a comfort to know that within everyone is a life force. That life force is the peace, joy, and courage we see in little children. As adults, it is mostly covered over with complex thoughts, relationships, and responsibility, but it is still, thankfully, present. This life force is not our personal possession. But we get to experience it, as long as we are here. Why not become familiar with its good company?

I am not saying that getting to a wonderful place for dying is easy. It has not been for me. There is a multi-headed dragon of death—these are the fears we need to slay. These can take various forms. For example, one fear is that our being, our consciousness, will cease to exist as our body shuts down and returns to dust. Another fear is that at the end of our days, we will feel our life is empty of meaning, purpose, and enjoyment—the nihilism of depression. Another head of the dragon of death is the idea that we will encounter some kind of divine punishment for our mistakes. These fears can generate anger and drive stress reactions that separate us from the wisdom we need. Fortunately, we have the ability to move around all the obstacles we might encounter. We shall see in the stories in this book how we can behead this dragon, a wonderful triumph of the human spirit.

Each section of this book highlights stories that illustrate the five necessary understandings to navigate a safe, comfortable, and peaceful departure. Accepting you are going to leave is the first step. This allows you to become aware of the choices to do it in your own way. Simplicity can guide these choices to be yourself in the last chapters of your life. We can resolve regrets while living so we can be free to feel the goodness of the life force. It can and will be there with you in your last breaths, just as it was in your first breaths, whether you are aware of it or not. This life force is the source of peace and can be your legacy.

In Brief: The Five Understandings

1. **Accept Death.** We have a great desire to deny that we will leave this life one day, but accepting this reality gives us

strength. If we do not accept and come to peace with this reality, it triggers useless stress reactions. As a young doctor, I wanted to fight death with the power of medicines and surgeries. When I succeeded, I felt great; when I lost I felt bad. But inevitably, every human eventually loses the fight. Accepting this truth opens us up to myriad benefits of comfort and inner peace.

Albert Einstein said that we need to decide whether this universe is kind or not. Accepting that dying is as natural as birth gives us the perspective necessary to enjoy each day. We can accept the reality of each day as a gift and choose to make the effort to enjoy each day. For good reason, we have the unique ability as human beings to recognize our mortality. We have good reason to choose to understand and make the best of our lives. As you will see in some of these stories herein, it is never too late to do this.

2. **Do It Your Way.** To some extent you have choices about the circumstance of your dying. Safety, comfort, and kindness are necessary, so some planning is needed. You can make decisions in your favor to disengage from life at the pace you want rather than be subjected to lifestyles, habits, or medical procedures that often cause more suffering or less consciousness in your final days. If you do not take responsibility for decisions, others will make them for you. Family, friends and especially health professionals may not be able to see things through your eyes. You are the one best equipped to make those decisions if you have the conscious capacity to do so.

3. **Embrace Simplicity.** This understanding puts you in the position to keep things simple as you approach your departure. Appreciating the elegance and grace of simplicity is an artistic and human effort right up to and through the end. Rather than undergoing futile medicine in which doctors go to all ends to preserve your life at great cost with little benefit to you, you may wish to experience death with consciousness and dignity in home hospice or a hospice facility surrounded by family and friends. In effect, the efforts of kind, conscious doctors and hospice nurses are valuable, but when the medical industry becomes unconsciously reactive and unfeeling, it is dangerous.

4. **Resolve Regrets.** No one has ever completed all the items on their bucket list. In resolving regrets, we can appreciate all that we did and let go of all we did not do or become. When it comes to lingering animosities and hatreds, forgiving and feeling gratitude can be easier than we might think, especially when there is not so much time left to dwell on personal problems with others others and even our own past actions. Forgiving is about letting go of bad feelings, not condoning any harm that has been done.

5. **Discover Peace.** If we can accept the reality of dying and not be afraid, we can learn to reflect on the purpose and meaning of our life. Before we depart is the time to discover and cherish whatever it is that sustains our existence and is with us to the very end — and perhaps beyond. There is peace there.

These understandings comprise what I have learned from the many trips I have made with my patients and friends down that last corridor to their departure. I will illustrate each understanding with stories about the deaths of those patients and friends that I have attended to. I seek to inspire you and drive home the deep meaning of each of the five understandings. In relating their stories, I honor them and acknowledge the impact they have had on my life and my work as a medical doctor. These patients came as gifts to me and their stories have been gifts to many more patients. Hopefully they are gifts to you whether you are yourself the person waiting to depart or the caregiver of another.

UNDERSTANDING 1

Accepting Death

WE HAVE A GREAT DESIRE TO DENY THAT WE WILL leave this life one day, but accepting this reality gives us strength.

The first thing we need to understand is the necessity to accept that we are going to someday die, hopefully later rather than sooner. Every human body is temporary. But in the depth of our being is something that does not die. Facing death is easier if we are on friendly terms with this life force, this spark within that does not die. This is not an intellectual belief. We have to enlist the wisdom of our heart. This peaceful expression of the life force is pure and so perfect, it does not need to evolve. Indeed peace and joy in a child looks the same as the peace and joy expressed by some of us as we depart. This is our evolutionary potential, but we need to accept our physical, mental, and emotional mortality to know this aspect of ourselves.

If we do not engage in a meaningful way with the fact that we are surely going to depart from here, we end up in fear, frustration, or pain. These are the triggers for the stress system menu of actions to occur, which include either the fight, flight, freeze, or gathering together with others for mutual defense. Getting stuck in these instinctive reactions to dying is not practical. You can only fight so much before it hurts your ability to deal with the realities of dying. As for flight, where can you run or hide from death? Freezing in the face of death is a death itself. As for gathering, will all your friends and family be able to protect you from the inevitable?

The advances of modern medicine, plus improvements in sanitation, can treat and even prevent many causes of death. This is really good. There are also those who think that reverse engineering the human body to not die for a really long time is possible. Some even dream of the permanent denial of death.

The truth is, there is a great strength in the acceptance of death. One day, we all will go. It frees us of useless stress responses so we may discover what we really need to know. Most of us can remember and perhaps reflect on the time that we almost died from an accident, illness, or our own poor decision making. When we survived, we felt relieved and exuberant to realize we did not die.

Acceptance is the mother of understanding. It is better to understand before the end is near so you have a reflective space to make wise decisions and let peace find you sooner rather than later. The stories in this section are very close to my heart because these experiences allowed me to accept that death can be as amazing and as transformative as birth.

Whenever someone tells me that someone they love has recently died, I express my condolences, and then ask, was it peaceful? "Yes, it was peaceful," is the most usual response. That peace is not environmental or provided by others; it is an expression of a reality at the core of human existence.

The great Chinese sage Confucius said, "You will not understand your death unless you understand your life." In this life, there is work to do to come to a place of understanding where we can leave with a final, beautiful exhale.

In the following pages, I will share stories from patients I worked with on the East Coast in Bethesda, Maryland as well as patients I encountered much later, during my 25 years of practice in Westlake Village, California.

1. Our heroic journey from birth to death

"EVERYONE WHO HAS BEEN PRESENT AT A BIRTH, please raise your hand."

"Now, everyone who has been present at a death please raise your hand."

These are my requests when I conduct a training for hospice staff and volunteers. Then I ask those people who raised their hands for both occasions another question: "What is the difference between the feeling at a birth versus at death? Not the thoughts or emotions or imagination, just the feeling?"

It takes a minute or so for each person to reflect and consider what to say to this odd question. I carefully watch the faces of those few people among all the other puzzled people. A small shy smile and even gentle laughter appear in the faces of those who have been present at both arrival days and departure days. There is a sense of being present for a great mystery, something awesome and beyond description: the appearance and departure of life in a human body.

I ask one more question to the hospice professionals in the group: "What stays and goes with you at the end?"

These are experienced people who have witnessed many departures. We quickly agree that nothing material goes with you — not your money, car, friends, or even a relative. Certainly not your body, which will be buried, burned, or even perhaps composted.

What about memories, do they go with you? Some in the audience think so, but I point out that memories exist in our brains and for some of us as we get older, they disappear as brain cells die off. In the case of a stroke or dementia, memories are quickly erased. Then I ask them to again forget about what they think and instead pay attention to what they have observed in the departures they have seen.

The answers to this question are always the same. We arrived with these qualities and perhaps we can love, contentment, kindness, and gratitude. If this seems farfetched, perhaps you have yet to witness it. We arrived with these qualities; when the conditions are right, perhaps we can also depart in the company of these qualities.

We have a clear picture of the tranquil baby in the arms of the tired, blissful mother. We can enjoy and depend on the ability of an infant or a small child to be peaceful, joyful, playful, and content. In fact, these innate qualities of an infant allow us to know they are okay. The coos and big eye smiles reward us for all the hard work it takes to care for them.

Many of us who work in hospice have enjoyed the same sense of well-being, watching a person depart gracefully in peace. A job well done — we all feel that.

Birth is a heroic journey for the infant and mother. You certainly were the hero of your arrival, and it was quite a show. You started out as one tiny cell, the union of one sperm and one egg in your mama's fallopian tube or perhaps a test tube. Against all odds, you developed in the safety of the womb. The day came and you departed from that luxurious nutrient-rich liquid residence. You faced many challenges — breathing air, adapting to gravity, being at the mercy of a changing environment. Instinctively, you connected to the force of life, and the force was with you. Life does not happen unless a force is exerted within that tiny infant.

A neonatal specialist at Duke Medical School told us medical students in the most memorable lecture of my four years at Duke that "our first breath is arguably the most strenuous effort we can ever make as a human being." He compared the force that an infant exerts to push all the fluid out of the more than 500 million individual air sacs to the power of a rocket ship at lift off and breaking away from the gravitational pull of the Earth. No wonder we are tired after our birth.

In witnessing a birth and a child's first breath, we become the carriers of a piece of their story. Similarly, in witnessing a person's last breath, we become carriers of a piece of their story. We carry this imprint and can share it with friends, family, and even future ancestors. Each person's story can become part of the fabric we weave — the golden threads of our humanity. Leaving a legacy of dignity and peace at our exit from the stage of this world is a noble goal worth embracing.

Last breaths can be as enjoyable as the first ones; there is just a different effort to be made. Can I let go of everything here on earth? *Everything?* It sounds simple but depends on what we focus on. Ideally, we embrace the energy of life and stay with it as long as it feels good. Sometimes, gravity simply feels heavier and heavier as we age our way out. And eventually, we simply cannot carry our vessel of a body around any longer. Time to let it go.

We all wonder: what happens after departure? On the one hand, we know that the body will return to dust; this is certain. What happens to the energy of our life force though? Do we continue somewhere else? I do not know but I do know that when the time comes, I just want to embrace that energy and be open to what's next.

From the moment of our arrival, that force has been with us beneath the surface of life — reliable and independent of everything else. At departure, it gives us the strength and courage to let go of everything. We can be with that force no matter where it takes us. Our departure can be graceful and peaceful. This can be our final gift to others as well as to ourselves.

2. A Good Place to Die

A NEATLY DRESSED INDIAN MAN TAPPED ME ON THE shoulder to make sure he had my attention. His words, "Doctor! Come now!" were delivered with a thick accent. I jumped to my feet and followed him without pausing to consider how this stranger even knew I was a doctor. He had summoned me from amongst the nearly 500 foreign guests at a huge gathering in Delhi, India. I was there to listen to the young teacher, Prem Rawat, talking about self-knowledge and inner peace. I had just put 5,000 miles between myself and my medical internship "year of death," hoping to heal from the trauma of my years of study and all-night shifts at the hospital. I wasn't at the gathering to practice medicine that day, and I hadn't identified myself as a doctor, but these three little words were my summons to duty.

Just out of training, I wondered what kind of problem I was about to encounter. We walked quickly through a colorful sea of Indian people at the outdoor conference center where the principal speaker was giving his final talk of the day. As the man led me through the crowd, I had plenty of time to notice all my feelings: fear, urgency, a crazy sense of responsibility, and anxiety.

Carrying the weight of my fears — and the hope that I could help — I was led to a large tent. Lying motionless in the center of a small crowd of people was my new patient. As I knelt next to him, I immediately realized that he had no need for my care.

He was dead, though his body was still warm.

I had all kinds of irrational thoughts. Should we have done something to save him just now or at least should I have made a show of doing CPR? Could I have revived him if we had walked faster? Was I guilty of some sort of neglect? Did I make a mistake? I looked around at the calm, reassuring faces above me as I knelt by the body. Perhaps nobody had done anything wrong. It was reassuring, soothing even, to feel the response of his friends and family. It was strange not to see the drama, confusion, fear, and blame I'd become accustomed to in my hospital.

"What did he die from?" people in the crowd asked.

They can't be serious, I thought. They knew he was dead long before I showed up. We would need an autopsy to be sure, but I realized that they just wanted some kind of explanation for the sudden death of their friend. Perhaps any explanation would do. So with doctorly authority and a furrowed brow I offered, "He died of a heart attack."

My statement did the trick. Animated conversation and gratitude for this news circulated in the room. Everyone was very satisfied — heart attack, good. With this explanation the small crowd seemed even happier. I was truly amazed, puzzled, and a little amused by the childlike innocence and happiness around me. This was a totally new experience.

He just died. How could this be good? "Why is everyone happy?" I inquired. Their attitudes were further afield than I could imagine.

"This is a nice place for him to die," someone kindly explained in good English. "He was among his family and friends, and he was understanding something wonderful about life; it was a good time for him to die."

This simple statement confronted all the dread, futility, and terror I had felt around the reality of a death during my five years of medical training. We were taught all that was known about the human body from the perspective of treating, curing, and preventing illness. We weren't taught how to deal wisely with the facts of dying and death. There was no academic lecture, seminar, or bedside teaching, no conversation over a coffee or beer to help us understand the meaning of death. Death was simply the end of our medical efforts, like a missed birdie putt on the 18th hole of the golf course.

Walking back toward the main stage, the doctor in me felt profoundly disoriented and challenged, but there was some relief and hope — maybe I could successfully practice medicine without the dark shadow of death always present, ready to eat me. I had to ask, could there really be a good death?

Before leaving India on that trip, I stayed on a houseboat on the Ganges River in Varanasi with an incredible group of people, a dance troupe called the Rainbow Gypsies. We were living right next to the stairs leading down to the Ganges, called the ghats. Day and night, right in front of us, dead bodies were piled on heaps of wood and burned. We also watched here and there the odd body that would float down the river.

People traveled great distances to die there because it is considered a really good place to die. The streets were filled with calm, tolerant sick people and beggars. Right next to the disabled beggars were vendors selling the most wonderful sweets, filling the early winter air with an enticing array of unfamiliar smells. The sweet warmth of life was there right next to the cold sadness of death. The comparison did not feel contradictory in the narrow streets of the holy city. Death was not separate from everyday life. Witnessing it day after day, I came to realize that there is nothing odd about death.

In Benares, I began looking for gifted healers. There were many such healers that I heard about and went on a mission to find. Each time I got close, a wise Indian elder would ask me why I wanted to meet a healer. I thought I might learn from such a person and improve my ability to help patients. In no uncertain terms, they informed me that these are gifts and cannot be taught or passed on. They encouraged me to learn to prevent illness.

3. Mr. V: Death—inevitable. Suffering—optional.

UPON RETURNING TO PRACTICE MEDICINE IN A suburban U.S. hospital, I was still singed by the flames of the dragon of death. For me, the image of death in American medicine was indeed a terrible dragon one hopes to never meet. This dragon has many heads reflecting our big fears.

- Will I cease to exist after death?
- What is going to happen when I die?
- Was my life worth anything (futility)?
- Did my life have any meaning?
- Will I be abandoned and alone?
- Will I be punished for my bad choices?
- Will I suffer unbearable physical pain?

These are the obstacles to a peaceful departure, a far cry from the simple ideal I had witnessed in India, where death was part of everyday life and could even be joyful. When you see something often, it diminishes in its ability to make you fearful.

The hospital where I practiced was in Bethesda, Maryland, near my general practice and across the street from the National Institutes of Health, which in turn is across the street from the Bethesda Naval Hospital where the President of the United States receives healthcare. In the early 1970s, it was customary for younger doctors to take on patients who had been admitted to the community hospital from the emergency room if they did not have a primary care doctor.

This is how I came to be Mr. V's doctor. Our journey together between life and death quieted my fear that death is just a never-ending darkness and gave me a deeper meaning to accepting death. Remembering that we die brings us strength and has the effect of making one more appreciative for each day we have to enjoy life. This is a simple, profound, universal understanding.

Mr. V was wiry and muscular, with a full head of jet-black hair and a penchant for arm-wrestling with his sons. He seemed more youthful than his 50-something years. A man of action par excellence, he approached his work as a pest exterminator with zeal. He was a ruthless killer of all manner of ants, bugs, and rodents. He was also extraordinarily goodhearted — the type of man you could call at 4:00 a.m. to help with a blocked toilet. He drove himself hard but possessed seemingly boundless vitality.

The heart attack that brought him to the emergency room of the hospital came as a complete surprise to him as well as to his consulting cardiologist, Doctor Kenner. He had no risk factors for heart disease, except perhaps his hyperactive way of being. The damage to his heart seemed mild, and given his general good health, we were all optimistic that he could resume his active life.

After doing well in the coronary care unit for a few days, Mr. V was moved to a regular hospital bed with less nursing supervision and care. In those days, there wasn't much to be done in the way of treatment besides bed rest so that damaged heart muscles could heal.

But Mr. V simply could not keep still. If his wife or sister came to visit, he'd move chairs for them. If he wanted something that was across the room, he'd go and get it. No amount of warning or stern talk from the cardiologist could alter his behavior. Dr. Kenner, a brilliant, kind, experienced cardiologist wanted to sedate Mr. V for a few days with Valium to calm him down. He refused, promising us he would stay still. But to rest was not in Mr. V's character. Later that week he was back in the coronary care unit with a new heart attack and was now mortally wounded.

Over the next week, Mr. V endured a series of cardiac arrests — more than 20 in all. Each episode was a life-and-death battle. Yet somehow, each time his heart stopped, we were able to shock it back into action and Mr. V emerged victorious, holding onto life.

I developed a strong rapport with this kind, soft-spoken man. I was struck by the calmness he exuded throughout these ordeals. Mr. V didn't have a philosophical or religious bone in his body, yet he confided that during his recent brushes with death, he had experienced a profound feeling of tranquility, love, and light that had shifted his perspective.

"Y'know, Doc," he told me, "If I'm going to be damaged, let me go. I don't want to live my life as a crippled person." He then made a singular statement, "I don't have any fear at all." I was astounded that this invincible warrior, whose hold on life was so tenacious, could also be so accepting and fearless about death.

During this time I also came to know his wife and his sister. As sincere Christians, they worried that if Mr. V died before he accepted Jesus, he might not go to heaven. They tried relentlessly to "reform" Mr. V, and even attempted unsuccessfully to enlist me in their efforts.

Remarkably, Mr. V recovered from all these cardiac events with his body and mind intact. Yet life was not going to be the same for him. In the months that followed, we would talk from time to time and there was always frustration and deep sadness when he spoke of his increasing physical limitations. My efforts focused on urging him to explore his own inner life through contemplative reading and reflection. He was not interested in this. The notion of an inner life was as remote for him as my experiences in India, which I insisted on sharing with him.

Eventually, Mr. V had another heart attack and was hospitalized yet again. Once more he bounced back, to the great amazement of the staff, with whom he was by now a favorite. On the third day of his hospitalization, I dropped by to see him in the late afternoon on my way home. Typically, I saw him during my morning hospital rounds as I tended to the psychological needs of my patients, and his cardiologist, Dr. Kenner, would see him throughout the day and at night if necessary. My spontaneous stopping by that afternoon felt very social, an expression of affection for this wounded warrior.

"So, Doc, am I gonna be able to do more now?" he asked wistfully. I hoped he was being sarcastic. As gently as I could, I told him he had sustained more heart damage and would be able to do even less than before. As he absorbed this news, I noticed that, rather than looking disappointed, he appeared uncharacteristically reflective. For the first time, the invincible Mr. V seemed to be in touch with—and accepting of—his own mortality.

He then asked me if I really believed that inner contentment was part of the purpose of life. And for the first time, he listened with interest as I spoke from my heart about this subject.

I told him that I saw two purposes to life. One is to create a beautiful life on an external level; the other is to feel the contentment and serenity that comes from connecting with the divine within our hearts, not necessarily by believing in a religion like his family wished he could do. I told him that peace is looking for us, just waiting to be enjoyed when we simply become still.

Mr. V didn't say much, but I could see he was resonating with my words in a way he never had when we'd talked before. His face relaxed into joyful peace and our mutual frustrations seemed to evaporate. I left rather exhilarated and somehow hopeful.

That night, I got a call around midnight from the coronary care unit asking me to come to the hospital right away. The head nurse said it was about Mr. V and I must come immediately. I protested. It was Dr. Kenner's responsibility to call the shots in the coronary care unit. They knew that, so why call me? They were adamant, insisting I come to the hospital immediately. Puzzled and worried, I drove the short distance to the hospital. Upon entering the coronary care unit, three or four nurses stood together to greet me. When I asked what was going on, one of them simply said: "He's gone."

I naturally asked what they had done — had they shocked him, injected this or that medicine into him, per Dr. Kenner's advice? With that question, three of the four nurses became more silent and fearful. I asked again and one of them said, "Nothing. We did nothing." What! The coronary care nurses saw on the monitor that the heart of a patient stopped — and they did nothing. The fire department comes to your burning house and they do nothing. This was a very big deal, to do nothing. They expected me to be understandably very upset and angry.

In the silence, I recalled my conversation with Mr. V that afternoon and the peace that our conversation had so clearly brought him. I also remembered how, during his sojourn of twenty resuscitations in that same unit with the same nurses a year earlier, he had told me that he was not afraid to die. In fact, I had promised him then that if he was terribly damaged, we would let him go. I like to think that those nurses who also cared deeply for Mr. V somehow had the good sense to let him go. He was already too damaged to enjoy any more life. I told them about our profound afternoon conversation. They felt better. Somehow, it was right.

Sun Tzu is said to have written, "The wise warrior avoids the battle." I like to think the invincible Mr. V had recognized a power even more implacable than his own and had laid down his sword at last.

What is the power of life that we rely on 100 percent of the time? Each breath we take is a gift from this gentle, kind power. It is not something we can control, so it is best embraced and enjoyed. The human body is perishable and designed to be recycled at some time. The power of life, on the other hand, is felt to be continuous — perhaps best described as infinite, unchangeable, and beyond intellectual understanding. A felt reality.

Mr. V helped me step beyond my own anxieties surrounding death. He allowed his hopes to be redefined and redefined until finally his time was up. The vehicle of his body became a shell, unable to go anywhere. Finished. He was liberated from his prison of inactivity into a tranquility that was palpable to all of us present at that midnight hour in the Suburban Hospital Coronary Care unit. Our hearts were alive with gratitude for the fearless Mr. V.

Now I knew with certainty, for the first time, that while death is inevitable, suffering is optional, even in an American hospital.

4. Joe: Can we know when it's over?

JOE PETERS WAS A RUGGED, HANDSOME, AND NOW elderly farmer. In his normal life, you wouldn't catch him without his cowboy hat on, busy wielding some kind of tool with his large, weathered hands. He came to the ER in Bethesda one evening with a serious stroke that had fully paralyzed the right side of his body.

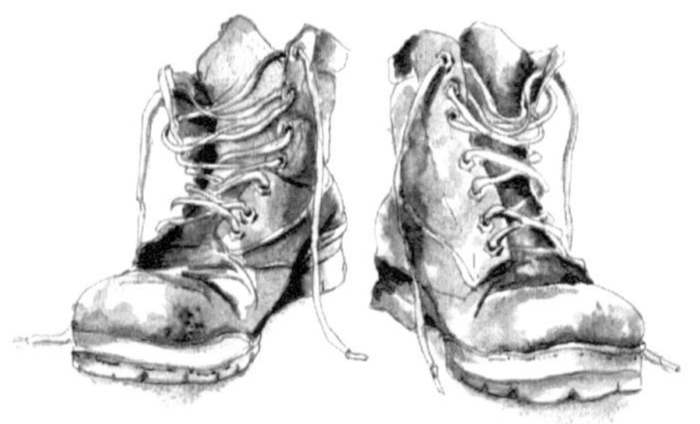

Joe became my new patient. Before going to see him, I checked with the nurses. They told me he didn't know he was in the hospital and was carrying on as if he were somewhere else. He had a large, loving family of biblical proportions, and they kept his room lively. He was clearly the patriarch, a firm but kind task-master. No one in the family, including his wife, seemed capable of confronting his massive denial that his life had changed. He could not move the right side of his body at all and he, quite likely, would be bed-bound forever.

The hospital staff and I appeared foolish to him. He asked me why I was talking to him and not doing the work he had assigned to me. He appeared to think it was early morning and he was standing on the front porch of his farmhouse giving everyone, including me, assignments for the day. This didn't change throughout this hospital stay.

Joe wasn't in danger of dying immediately nor was he really suffering because he wasn't aware of what was going on. Perhaps he could have recovered some mobility, but he wouldn't cooperate with physical therapy.

Hospitals don't like to keep people when there is nothing to be done and insurance companies don't like to pay hospital bills once the acute care is over. I hoped the day wouldn't come when we would have to sedate Joe and send him to a nursing home. Nobody wanted to steer Joe's tractor down that bumpy road.

Late one night, after taking care of a new admission, I went into his room on a whim. No one else was visiting him that night and so he was asleep. I took this moment and I started talking to him as if he were were awake and fully present. It sounds strange, but given my previous experience with Mr. V, I couldn't think of a reason not to. I told him who I was, what had happened to him, and what I thought — simple and straightforward. I explained that we were never going to be able to get him back anywhere near to his pre-stroke self, that he might be a prisoner of his bed from then on.

I explored the idea that at some point in our lives, like it or not, we must let go of the kind energy that has kept us alive, knowing that our body is no longer suited to support a life we could enjoy. It felt crazy to be talking to him about dying, but it also felt kind and generous to take this time to brief him without his family present. I do not remember my exact words, but I do remember telling him that he had a choice. I told him that no one had a clue what to do for him beyond keeping him alive in bed. I felt somehow that he understood what I was saying, and he was grateful for the information.

I told him that if his choice was to die, it would be quite okay because no one would want to see him in the prison of physical paralysis with no hope of parole. If he wanted to stay, we would continue to care for him as best we could. It was his choice. In that moment, I felt that I might be an angel of death if such a being were to exist, proposing a pathway for him to travel down to a good departure. But maybe I was being an angel of clarity, presenting him with the reality he was facing. It was only my experience with Mr. V and some study of near-death experiences that gave me the courage to talk with my sleeping patient about choice.

He died quietly at night a few days later. He never left his mental state of denial, so he had no conversations with his family about dying, though he could certainly feel their love and kindness. When he died, it was a relief for his family and the hospital staff because there was no good option for his care beyond the hospital. He no longer had the biological means to enjoy the active life he had known all his years. Perhaps I count this as a rather odd, graceful, peaceful departure. It eased my fears of failing a patient who is very ill.

The difference between reaching your natural end of life and being neglected or abandoned is very clear. When the body is shutting down of its own accord, the process feels settled and easy, dare we say, graceful. Nature is the great teacher about the timing of arrivals and departures. Medicine can assist but not dictate.

5. Valeria: Elegant acceptance

DECADES LATER BY WHICH TIME MY MEDICAL practice was in Southern California, I had a patient Valeria who a petite, elegant, brilliant artist who had severe high blood pressure. Her Latin passion for life, sparkling eyes, and easy laughter made her a very attractive woman. She was slender and fit, but in spite of numerous medical and naturopathic interventions, her blood pressure proved extremely difficult to control. As a result, she went into kidney failure and needed dialysis on a weekly basis.

The kidney failure had caused her bones to degenerate, and her body was disfigured due to multiple major spinal fractures. Her hips widened, she walked with a bent posture, her abdomen swelled, and she was easily fatigued. Her face remained quite beautiful and reflected the inner peace that was her saving grace in the midst of an unrelenting chronic, progressive disease.

Living with her physical illness for many years did not eclipse Valeria's love of life. She continued to paint and enjoy a rich social life, including attending performances of her husband's musical group. In my brief social interactions with her, she never failed to be kind, gentle, and uncomplaining. I admired her tenacity, strength, commitment, and courage.

For years I expected to hear from her husband, Alistair, that she had died. One day out of the blue, he called to request that I come by the hospital because Valeria wanted to see me. I was surprised since I only knew of her medical history secondhand (through my medical partner, who'd been treating her). Alistair told me that she had been in her usual state of health until a recent fall, which caused severe pain. She was being treated with opiates for rib fractures. Given the situation, I wondered what I could do for her.

That was when he told me: "Valeria has decided that she is done." His voice was quiet and unemotional.

"What does that mean, is she wanting to die right now?" I asked.

"Yes."

The scene in the hospital was of a tired, pale woman fighting to be comfortable, while her strong, calm husband looked overwhelmed. Delighted to see me, she greeted me with love and gratitude. Her brilliance of intellect and strength of heart were evident in her eyes and face, but her body looked worn out with not much life left. Bodies do wear out, like very old cars, and at some point they cannot be repaired. And even if you could patch up such a worn-out car you would never want to drive it. Bodies that are worn out and exhausted are simply unsuitable to be lived in, and it is better to let go.

I spoke with Alistair outside of the room while a nurse helped Valeria take care of a call of nature. I asked him if she had been in a lot of pain and fear when she said that she was done with living. "No, not at all," was his reply. She had been calm, clear-eyed, and sure: "Yes, I am done!" she had told him. He said this quite matter-of-factly, without obvious emotion. Remarkable, I thought, for such a champion of life to give up now. But why now?

Hearing Valeria confront the nurses, insisting that the blood she was waiting for should have been given hours earlier, I understood something of Valeria's strength in getting what she needed medically. Feisty behavior in the hospital is one explanation for Valeria's longevity. Sometimes it takes the voice of a lion to get one's needs met. Doctors may know more about the diseases and treatments, but you know more about your own body if you pay attention. That's why it's so important to trust yourself and speak up.

The specialists attending Valeria were not readily available in the midst of the COVID-19 pandemic. Fortunately, Alistair and I found the case manager in her office. She shared the clinical picture including MRIs, X-rays, and blood test results. All the vertebrae in her back had extensive fractures due to metabolic bone disease resulting from ten years of kidney failure and dialysis.

I had never seen such devastation of the bones of the spine and wondered how she managed to be mobile at all. There was also a mention of possible metastatic cancer in her bones. An oncology consult suggested a bone biopsy. We all laughed at the absurdity of a dying woman having a bone biopsy to treat a cancer with chemotherapy or radiation. Either treatment would kill her very quickly. We wondered if the oncology consultant had even seen her. If he did, he would not have made such a suggestion. This is a danger in any hospital stay: uninvolved, aggressive consultants making off-the-wall suggestions based on one or two scans they review, and not seeing the patient as a whole person. Once these random suggestions appear in a patient's chart, the treating doctor may feel compelled to act on them because of medical legal fears.

Alistair told the case manager that his wife had chosen to discontinue treatment. What was needed now was to transfer her to palliative care or hospice. The case manager was wonderful and immediately explained what arrangements needed to be made for hospice care at home.

While Alistair was busy with the case manager, I returned for a private talk with Valeria. I trusted Alistair's understanding of her choice, but I wanted to confirm it for myself. This is what a doctor wants to do: see it, hear it, and decide himself or herself.

I did not ask Valeria if she was ready to die; rather I asked if she was finished with dialysis, for now and forever. Her response was crystal clear and serene—yes, done forever. She knew that without dialysis, her death would occur in a few days, certainly less than a week. I appreciated the certainty and peace in her gaze, and she appreciated my unquestioning acceptance. The intimacy of that moment expanded our ability to know that her flight was waiting: her time had come.

How does a doctor know whether to agree with the patient or to counsel and convince them to fight on in spite of a temporary setback? It is due to training and perspective that a doctor can see more clearly than the patient whether a particular moment in a disease is temporary or not. Although the patient is discouraged or frustrated, the doctor's hopefulness can inspire the patient to find the courage to continue. But in this case, Valeria had been fighting heroically and, I thought, she had been cultivating the peace in her heart, preparing for the time to surrender to that peace and let go of the fight. She had been successful in preparing for this very moment.

With newly fractured ribs, Valeria would be in pain and even more immobilized than she had been. But people can adapt to less mobility and pain can be controlled. So, was it right for me to simply accept her desire to quit her ten-year fight? Her brain and spirit were still intact. How could I know how to help in this situation? Was she asking me to help her explain her decision to her husband and doctors who had also been fighting for her and might not be ready to give up? Is that why she called for me to support her departure? How could I know if this was the right thing for her? How could I know for certain? Medicine is based on science, but crucially requires the art of knowing the individual physically, mentally, and socially.

Carl Jung, the Swiss psychiatrist, described four ways of knowing. One is through our senses. We see, hear, smell, taste, and touch to know. We can also know by thinking, and by intuition (our so-called gut feelings), and finally we can know by feeling. Feeling can seem elusive because it is not an emotion. Feeling is of the heart.

In the stillness and tranquility of the heart, we have the chance to feel the gift of clarity. Clarity is a gift because it does not come from the realm of thought or concepts or belief or righteousness or fear. It is a pure expression of our ability to understand what is true in any important situation. Clarity is free from the wide ocean of coulds and shoulds. In clarity, there is no feeling of fear or compulsion. Clarity is a safe harbor or a smooth horizon.

It has taken me years of witnessing others' adventures at the end of life, as well as much reflection, to understand the essential and necessary meaning of clarity, clarity is a safe harbor and a smooth horizon. I guessed this was why Valeria summoned me for her exit. We talked about dignity in dying and this is what I saw for Valeria. Dignity has the strength of peacefulness, acceptance, and certainty. It is a valuable thing for a patient to feel. It gives a doctor more confidence and security in the decisions being made for the care of that person. The more solid the commitment of a person to find real clarity, the better the relationship between them and the doctors. I felt fortunate to be part of Valeria's command performance.

When I returned the next afternoon, Valeria had received her transfusion and she looked much better. Her facial color was back and now that her pain was stabilized, she was more animated in her expressions and conversation. We briefly revisited her decision to forgo further treatment; she now had an even greater depth of certainty. She exuded a delight in life, and a compelling stillness. I was excited to see how these next days would unfold. Would it be possible for Valeria to fly away in a deepening peace and passionate love of life?

"I need to go home today." Valeria looked at Alistair and said this forcefully, with all of her steely will.

This was late Friday afternoon, a difficult time to get things done. Alistair assured her that he could get her home the next morning. Her tone and look caused me to mirror her strength and tell Alistair — in no uncertain terms — she must go home now, not later. I used my power as a doctor and told him that this was an absolute medical necessity.

Poor Alistair — a gentle artist, a maker of wood sculpture and furniture, he knew how to get the best out of the wood through his patient and exacting labors of love. Now this reticent, cautious man of reflection, a calm Scotsman, and not one to rush decisions, was outgunned. His wife and doctor friend were saying, do this tonight, do it now.

The next day I saw Valeria at her home. She was lying in a hospital bed — her own mattress on top of the hospital mattress — looking pleased and happy after a restful night's sleep. Her gratitude for the quick action was immense, and Alistair was also grateful. Hospitals are necessary for the use of technology and intensive nursing care. But for rest, recuperation, and less technical or intensive care, they are a disaster.

There is a hierarchy of care in hospitals that might surprise a novice patient and their family. The most important person in the hierarchy is the doctor. Their needs and wishes are always the priority. The second most important people are the nurses, then ancillary personnel like X-ray techs and, last of all, the patient. That is just how it is. Valeria knew well that home was a sweet balm for her body, mind, and heart. Home was a place where she could be the top priority, as was needed for her last days to be rich with good medicine.

Over the next few days we witnessed a dance of love such as I had never seen before. I thought I had already written all the stories needed to convey the understandings that are essential and sufficient to make the possibility of a graceful and peaceful departure a reality. Then along came Valeria's request for my care, and she showed me there was one more thing to understand. The final understanding is to cultivate what stays with you up until the final breaths. Does this peace accompany the being once the body ceases to live? I do not know for sure, but it seems to. If we had a video of the bliss and unstoppable expression of love coming so sweetly from Valeria in those last two days of crystal clarity, no one would question the reality of what was being experienced.

It is never too late for the love of life to grow. The experience was contagious and, as I write about this, I am drawn back into that beautiful dance of clarity and love. At one point, she said, "I never knew that the divine love is completely nonjudgmental and just wants to fill all of our hearts." Another time she said, "Yes, this life is a dream, an illusion. The reality is beyond imagination." She was amazingly kind and hospitable to visitors. At one point she scolded Alistair for not offering me the really good snacks and beverages that their friends were consistently bringing. I ate well during my visits.

During those last few days of life, Valeria called her family in South America. Alistair described those calls as transformational for her and her family members. I knew little of her family difficulties, except that they had been traumatic. Apparently the richness of her love and joy allowed for all kinds of forgiveness and expressions of love between them. Alistair emerged from those days strong, solid, and ready for his next adventures.

A week after Valeria died, I invited Alistair to my home. Over dinner with my wife, Stella, he shared that while he felt waves of sadness and loss, they never obscured the love he felt for Valeria. That love, he told us, was not diminished by Valeria not being here physically any longer.

What I learned most from this adventure is the necessity for clarity in decision-making. Clarity affects all our thoughts, emotions, and actions. But to live or to die, this clarity is of a different order than the usual clear thinking of everyday life. This clarity is the difference between creating pain, fear, and suffering for someone, and providing the comfort, understanding, and support for something wonderful to happen within the person as they transition between physical life and whatever happens to us when we die.

No one (except for someone in severe depression or despair) wants to die, but the wise among us know when it is time to die. Valeria had the courage to know when it was time. It must be similar to the courage we need as newborns when we let go of our life in the womb and make the profound effort to take that first breath and become an independent being. Letting go of life on Earth to venture into the unknown certainly requires the same courage and strength. At some point there is no choice — it is time to go.

Another moment of clarity was Valeria's recognition of her need to leave the hospital that evening and not the next day. Alistair was shocked because he had to do a lot quickly to make that happen. Fortunately, he could hold onto the clarity of Valeria's understanding with my support.

A third instance of clarity occurred when Valeria's body went into the biology of what we call in the hospice craft, "active dying." This is a peculiar term for outsiders, but actually quite accurate. The dying that is psychological and social has been the major subject of this story, but there is also the physical. At some point, the body insists on doing its own dying process, which involves the selective shutting down of all the life-supporting systems that were committed to keeping us alive. This shutting down can be a bumpy road with variations in blood pressure, heart rate, respiration, muscle activity, and anxiety. This is where the hospice nurses can be so valuable. With medications and caring strategies, they can smooth out the bodily reactions so that the peaceful nature of pure consciousness is unobscured.

When I suggested to Alistair that we should get the hospice nurse to come quickly, he was surprised. He and I and various friends had been appreciative of the bliss and lack of suffering, pain, or despair in Valeria's final days. Why threaten the sanctuary of their cozy home with a medical stranger? This is a completely understandable response. Some people might fear a hospice nurse will hasten death with excessive medications. And to be fair, sometimes the patient or their family actually want this because everyone is suffering. But such was not the case in this instance. In my experience, hospice nurses can help mitigate discomfort as the dying process becomes more biological than psychological or social. They are uniquely trained to do so.

In a way, these last days were the cherry atop a most elegant cake. The candle perhaps burned most brightly at the end for Valeria. During that time, Alistair read aloud some of the messages friends had written to her: expressions of sadness about her imminent death and admiration for her courage to let go, tributes to her strength, playful declarations of love, and all sorts of other random and lovely expressions. I was present when she dictated her response to her husband to be shared with her friends. With his permission (and I hope her pleasure) it is included in this portrait.

Perhaps we all get a glimpse of pure consciousness before our exit through the wall of death. Perhaps few of us have the passion in our lives to cultivate those seeds of joy, contentment, clarity, and love as the main event of life. Perhaps few of us get to dance so fully in our last days and hours as my friend Valeria.

Here is her message to all the friends who were wishing her well as they heard that she had decided to die after so many years of pushing through a deadly and disfiguring disease.

> I am honored to receive your beautiful words and expressions. I have no words to say that can capture my amazement that I could be loved so much, that you have learned from me. I wish you all the most beautiful life, full of presence and divinity. Each one of you is full of divinity. Each one of you that has crossed my life is such a gift. It is unbelievable how much love you have. Thank you, thank you. I wish I never hurt you if I did.
>
> I was waiting to come to a point where I had fully received and understood what I was given. I am in so much joy you would not believe it. I am just happy. I thought it was going to be sad and scary, but I have not felt a bit of that. I can't believe I am so happy. I am just happy. I wish you all the best. My time on Earth is done. All is well. All is well.

In a conversation with Alistair a few weeks after Valeria's death, I asked him about her farewell message, one line in particular;

"I was waiting to come to a point where I had fully received and understood what I was given." I wondered what that meant to him. He shared something he understood about that sentence: healing can continue into death.

Perhaps this is what Valeria was experiencing, the resolution of the traumatic experiences that had caused her to be less than herself. It does seem that the healing of trauma is a necessary part of being able to experience all the love and joy that is available to a human being. Perhaps not being able to accept all the riches within our being is the last obstacle to reaching the inner goal of a human life.

6. Sarah: Intuition and a close call sparks a new lease on life

SARAH WAS AN AMERICAN WHO HAD BEEN A PRISONER of war in a Japanese concentration camp in the Philippines during World War II. By the time she was my patient, she was gray, sullen, and very thin, seeming to live only by a force of will. She did not seem to have any love or joy in her life. It was painful to see her or talk with her. She lived on her own with lots of cats. The only time we ever saw her in our office was when she had infected cat bites and needed medicine. We guessed that she had some sort of pension and that she lived modestly by herself.

We were helpless to form any reasonable connection with her until she had an extraordinary near-death experience. She had come to the office without an appointment, suffering from a bad cold that turned out to be pneumonia. As she was frail and without home support, we admitted her to the hospital.

After a few days she was doing well, and although she did not interact with the hospital staff, she seemed grateful for the care. As usual, I saw her in the morning before my office hours. The lung specialist was satisfied with her progress, and there was talk of her leaving the hospital in a few days. At around 11:00 a.m. that very day, I was in my office when I had the sudden feeling that I had to get to the hospital right away to see my reluctant patient. An emergency visit to a patient in the hospital is really outside of medical protocols — there were plenty of doctors at the hospital: no one had called me to come immediately. It felt crazy, but it was such a profound intuition that I frantically drove there, leaving my staff and the waiting patients baffled. The 10-minute drive to the hospital seemed to take forever.

As I walked into her room, she stopped moving. We saw one another for a moment as her body shut down. She was in cardiac arrest, which we were able to quickly reverse. If I had not arrived at that time, none of the staff would have noticed because she was not hooked up to any monitors. My intuition to leave the office that day was a saving grace.

That moment — when I walked into the room and we saw one another — was the most conscious moment that we had ever had with one another. She needed brief intensive care to recover from the cardiac arrest and she left the hospital fully recovered.

The day that Sarah came to follow up in our office she had changed a little bit. Somehow, that connection she and I had saved her life. Even though her life still seemed dreadful, she appreciated our unrelenting medical care and love for her. She was not so eager to leave as when we treated her infected cat bites. She almost smiled at my nurse and receptionist.

About a year later, I had to tell her goodbye due to my own circumstances. The medical practice to which I belonged would still be there to take care of her, but I was leaving it so we would not see one another again.

Sitting with her in the privacy of my office, I felt sad telling her that I would no longer be her doctor. She smiled at me for the first time. Maybe she was going to be okay. My nurse and I watched her walk out, down the long corridor to the reception area. She started dancing. She was dancing a jig. She couldn't see us, so her joyful moves were just for her. It was a youthful, joyful moment of appreciation of life that I will always remember. Was it the near-death experience that caused a shift in her? Was facing death such a powerful tonic for life?

It was a most wonderful moment for all of us and left me feeling that she would indeed be okay. Sarah's numbness from her prolonged PTSD suffering had softened and allowed for at least one jig. Hopefully there were many more. She had not yet reached a place where she was good to go, and she had the ability to evolve. Cheers Sarah, love to you. Dance on.

7. Claudia: Trying on attitudes

CLAUDIA WAS A YOUNG WOMAN WHO CAME TO consult with me about her early morning panic attacks. She had been diagnosed with multiple sclerosis some months before I met her when she — as often happens with an initial MS attack — was suddenly struck with such profound weakness and numbness in her legs that she was unable to walk.

Her diagnosis was made in the hospital by a rather callous neurologist. Instead of talking with her and answering questions, he gave her a video about MS to take home. Fortunately, she was wise enough to consult another specialist. She was relieved to learn that her type of MS was not life threatening or as grim as the video had indicated. It could be treated successfully. She was looking at a normal life span with some handicaps. This was a relief, but this new information did not stop her nightly panic attacks. She was terrified of dying.

Her regular medical doctor prescribed tranquilizers for the attacks, but they left her feeling numb and drugged. She hoped that I would prescribe a vitamin or herbal supplement rather than another strong pharmaceutical. During the consultation, it became clear she had already tried just about everything I could think of from the shelves of health food stores.

She was a bright, successful young woman. I was surprised that her panic attacks, with their combination of sweating, breathlessness, racing heart, nausea, and a feeling of paralysis, had persisted for months after her initial scare. The cause was clear — she had been intimidated by her initial MS scare. Even though she knew she would have many decades of reasonable health in the shadow of MS, she was terrified of the possibility of death. So, it was not the disease that was causing her panic, it was the fear of a distant death. Puzzled, I asked her what she thought would happen when you die. Her eyes communicated what she could not say in words — pure, undiluted terror.

We cannot reason with terror. When it grips us we fight, run, freeze, or gather with others to feel safety in numbers. The stress system is powerful and easily funnels our attention into these biological responses rather than reasonable thinking. Claudia was in a freeze reaction. There is no way to fight or flee or gather with others in the face of an imagined death. I offered her the attitude exercise from *The Inner Game of Stress*, a book I had written with Tim Gallwey and Doctor Edd Hanzelik, my medical partner. This exercise can quickly allow someone to shift out of the stress system to a better state of mind and feeling.

An attitude is a settled way of thinking or feeling about someone or something, typically one that is reflected in a person's behavior even though the attitude is not conscious. Someone who has an attitude of fear or distrust will walk across a street to avoid passing a large, foreign-looking man on the same sidewalk, even though that person is kind and friendly. The person crossing the street has an attitude about large foreign-looking men. All of us have many rational or irrational attitudes; however if we're not aware of an irrational attitude, we cannot change it.

In the attitude exercise, you look at something that you know is very stressful and try on different attitudes as if you were trying on clothes. The idea is to choose an attitude that feels good, comfortable, and that suits you. It's not a question of what is right, correct, proper, or what pleases other people, but what feels comfortable and appealing to you. You can get playful and try on many attitudes before you find the one you like.

Claudia was hopeful at the idea of this exercise. Before we began it, I emphasized that some of our most firmly held attitudes are unconscious. The magic of this exercise is that when an attitude that inhibits your growth becomes conscious, there is an automatic attraction to a better attitude. We are all driven to evolve out of unnecessary suffering.

Initially, she was too anxious to consider describing an attitude to try on. I have a good imagination, so I just threw out suggestions. We imagined each attitude as a fine well-fitting dress of differing colors and fabrics that she was trying on in an upscale boutique in the company of a friend. The outfit she would finally select would feel elegant, comfortable, and attractive. It was a gift, so price was not a concern. She would wear it to a wonderful social event. Trying on clothes in such a context can only be fun and exciting if there are some that fit reasonably well. For some, this exercise might work better if they imagine they are taking different models of cars out for a test drive rather than trying on clothing.

So, Claudia tried on a few dresses:

When you die, if you have been good, you go to heaven.

This idea became a white sundress—she did not like it at all. The idea of going to hell for being bad was an uncomfortable black dress that did not feel good. Claudia did try on the orange and green dresses of karma and reincarnation for a while, and although she could wear them, they ultimately did not feel good either. As we were playing with the attitudes as dresses, she began to sit back, relax, and enjoy our indulgence in imagination.

When you die everything about you is annihilated and there is nothing at all.

Claudia exploded with anxiety as she became aware that this was exactly what her father insisted she believed during her childhood. He was a physicist who labeled those who thought differently as foolish and cowardly. This was the unconscious attitude that caused her terror. She couldn't fathom the idea of complete annihilation; neither could I.

My next suggestion relieved Claudia's panic.

Ever since you were born, a very subtle, gentle, and kind energy has been keeping you alive. Perhaps when you die, this energy is there to accompany you to whatever happens next.

Bingo! She loved and embraced that attitude. Now when she started to panic in the early morning hours, she would don this forest-green dress and relax back to sleep in the good company of the kind and gentle energy of her life.

I was her general doctor for about five years after this consultation. Her early morning terror never returned. Can it be that simple? At the end of life, the notion of what is right becomes very personal. The question you must ultimately ask yourself is, "What is the best choice for me in my circumstances?" As Shakespeare put it, "To thine own self be true, and it must follow, as the night the day, thou canst not then be false to any man." At the end of your life it is not necessary to please others — this is the last act in your play.

Even in the case of great demise with illnesses such as dementia, we can redefine and redefine and redefine until we let go of the expectations that a person functions the way we think they should. Our expectations of a baby and toddler and young child and teenager and young adult get redefined naturally as they progress. The end of life is no different, moving in the other direction back to our simplest possible nature.

If you don't like something, change it.
If you can't change it, change your attitude.
—Maya Angelou

8. Viktor Frankl and attitude

VIKTOR FRANKL WROTE "MAN'S SEARCH FOR MEANING" in 1946, chronicling his experiences in an Auschwitz concentration camp. A psychiatrist, he noticed that there were three different responses among the prisoners to the horror and extreme suffering in the camp. The first response was despair and collapse, waiting for and almost wanting death. Others responded by collaborating with the Nazi guards, doing favors and getting favors — sometimes to the detriment of other prisoners. The third group did not despair and did not compromise themselves with the Nazis. This group fascinated Frankl. He found that they were able to connect to a simple contentment and kindness.

I think this is the true nature of every human being. I have benefited many times from Frankl's observations when finding my patients immersed in suffering. The following words are from Frankl's writings:

> Our greatest freedom is our ability to choose our attitude. We who lived in concentration camps can remember the

men who walked through the huts comforting others, giving away their piece of bread. They may have been few in number, but they offer sufficient proof that everything can be taken from a man but one thing: the last of human freedoms — to choose one's attitude in any given set of circumstances, to choose one's own way.

UNDERSTANDING 2

Do It Your Way

THERE IS POWER IN KNOWING YOU CAN LEAVE ON your own terms. Ideally, you are in the drivers seat; you can take control of how you exit this life. If you do not take responsibility for making decisions, others will make them for you. Family, friends and especially health professionals often cannot see the meaning you ascribe to passing on through your eyes. You may suffer from their decisions.

Of course, when death comes suddenly, there will not be time to make your own decisions. This is why it it's important that you and your family, or whoever will see to the ending arrangements, has a clear vision of what you want and do not want.

Your decision to depart need not be about pleasing other people or the doctors who may want to keep you alive past your comfortable "shelf life" for their own reasons. Some of these reasons are not bad—like love, attachment, and fear of their grief. Other reasons are truly bad—like the greed of medicine, the pride of doctors, and the denial of your death among your family or friends. It takes courage to be true to yourself at any time in life. Steve Jobs' advice rings especially true here: "Your time is limited, so don't waste it living someone else's life."

We prepare for birth by considering a menu of choices and hiring the people that we want to care for us at this time of great vulnerability. Why not consider the same when thinking about a safe, comfortable, peaceful departure? Some people prefer to be at home no matter what; others prefer hospital or palliative care facilities. These are personal choices and they need to be respected. Flexibility is essential.

9. Sascha: The wisdom of a long life

ALL THE WINDOWS ARE FULLY OPEN, EMBRACING THE morning birdsong and the scent of orange blossoms. In a few hours they'll be shuttered again against the midsummer heat. With a broad smile, one-year-old Byron wakes, rubs his eyes, and sits up quietly between his parents. Gazing calmly from one sleeping parent to the other, he begins to giggle and clap his hands as he discovers his five-year-old sister asleep next to him. He leans in and tries to rouse her with his new favorite skill — kisses. With one eye open, his mother bears witness and revels in the moment. His giggly sounds are the blessed song lines of joy. Without thought, his inherent peace and joy is a blessing to those around him. This is a memory his mother Sushila wants to hold on to.

I met an elderly patient named Sascha who was a lot like Byron. He showed up unannounced at my office one fine morning in the fall. Mrs. Murphy, our front office assistant, insisted I come and see him immediately. She made the right call. This emaciated old man was struggling to breathe and he was clearly in pain, but Sascha's deep amber eyes burned with a passion to live.

We gave him oxygen in the waiting room, afraid to even move him to the consulting rooms. His daughter should have taken him straight to the ER, yet here he was, dying in my waiting room. It seemed death was taking him prematurely because of neglect.

He survived the short ambulance ride and was quickly admitted to the intensive care unit. He had pneumonia, which could have been easily treated with oral antibiotics at home if he had seen a doctor. Now his condition was critical. It would take a truly heroic effort to save him. Perhaps it was lack of money or genuine ignorance about how sick he was, but he had spent weeks very ill at home before he came for treatment. The passion for life in his eyes and the innocence and calm that we felt around him inspired the whole team.

The ace intensive care specialist in the Bethesda area was Dr. Elliot Goldstein. When we had a patient needing his expertise, he would usually consult briefly and leave orders for other doctors to carry through. He was so skilled at this that we usually didn't need him to see that patient again. When Dr. Goldstein first saw this man grasping for life with such dignity and passion, he was visibly moved and compelled to spend almost the whole night working to keep him alive.

He survived and was transferred out of intensive care where a new group of nurses, aides, and doctors came to appreciate him. Those same calm, passionate eyes now also emanated an unspoken gratitude: he seemed to appreciate every minute of consciousness, though he mostly slept. He was very weak and could barely talk, let alone stand up, but he was alive and grateful. We were all struck by his determination and contentment, like a newborn infant.

Once he was stable, it fell to me to figure out where he could go when he left the hospital, because the hospital was going to kick him out at a certain point. With really good care, it was possible he could live for some time, but if he went to a nursing home that his daughter could afford, we all knew they would not have the resources to take care of such a weak man. He couldn't go home. His daughter wasn't involved much with his discharge plan — her guilt over her neglect of him drove her away. So, the task fell to me.

Since no one could think of a possible discharge plan, I thought, why not ask the man in question? Maybe he had a nephew in Boston who could take care of him. As I walked toward his room that evening, I remembered advice I'd heard from a wise psychiatrist during a summer training program in San Francisco: If you're in front of a patient and you don't have a clue what to say, just stop, go inside, and then say whatever comes to you. Say it right from your heart. I stopped and took a moment before entering his room.

After saying hello and assessing his energy levels, what came out of my mouth was, "What do you want to do with the rest of your life?" It was an utterly absurd question, and I was afraid that he would laugh or cry. Instead, he perked up. With bright eyes, he spoke in a barely audible whisper. I will never forget his words. With tenderness, he said, "Toward the end of my life I've walked amongst people, and I haven't felt separate. I've felt the same. I want to be amongst people, and I want to be a blessing to people."

His ambition reminds me of the innocence and delight of young Byron upon waking, but with the wisdom of a long life.

I was so moved that I could hardly speak. He was exhausted, and I was no closer to figuring out what was next for him. I bid him good night and told him I would see him in the morning. Looking back, I wish that I had told him that for so many days his passion for life and his peacefulness had been a blessing to all of us.

The hospital floor where he was had been inspired and harmonious during his stay. But the next morning, it was transformed with bickering and fighting. He had died. Shocked, angry fingers pointed blame. Someone should have done something — he was not supposed to die after that heroic struggle.

I paused and reflected on this. Maybe death was instead a friend. This was a good death. He had no place to go, and he was at peace. He had not been afraid to choose his own path and embrace a new adventure. Blaming each other detracted from our ability to appreciate his legacy.

We shared our affection for him during an impromptu meeting. I told the staff about the previous night's conversation and the lack of a place for him to go when leaving the hospital. There was so little left of him physically. He was like a baby in a worn-out body. He needed only peace.

Somehow, he accomplished his dying wish right there, as if singing a sweet departing song before taking flight. He was amongst us, and he was a blessing. In all the years since then, his simple aspiration has protected me from feeling that death is a dragon of futility.

What does your picture of an ideal death look like? In our pictures of dying, we may see ourselves surrounded by loving family and friends, people appreciating our brilliant legacy of achievements, artistry, or some such idealist fantasy. Yet here was this man, completely isolated in a hospital. No family came to see him. We had no idea of his accomplishments or so-called legacy. Yet I am still moved by his legacy more than 40 years later.

As a well spent day brings happy sleep,
So, a life well used brings a happy death.
— Leonardo da Vinci

10. David: Love conquers fear

MY CLOSE FRIEND FOR FORTY YEARS, DAVID WAS A broad-shouldered towering man originally from Maine. He was blue eyed, handsome, and fit. As a graduate of Yale, he could have done many lucrative things, but he chose to work with non-profits. He was a facilitator of personal growth.

Most winters, David experienced bronchitis for a couple of weeks, but one year it lingered, and his breathing was compromised. A chest x-ray revealed pneumonia and a tumor in the lung. After a lengthy diagnostic work up, the specialists found a very aggressive lung cancer. It came as a shock to David, his partner, family, and friends, and was very difficult for me as his friend and doctor.

We chose the best oncologists at Cedars-Sinai in Los Angeles. David had surgery, followed by aggressive chemotherapy, but whatever they threw at it, nothing stopped the tumor's advance. David found himself with no weapons to fight it and no place to hide. His decline from robust health to profound disability was so abrupt that there was little time to grieve the loss of function. His energy to work, read, visit with friends, or even watch TV diminished rapidly. Just a few short months later, he could no longer walk or even sit up.

His partner of many years, Elisa, was a beautiful, bright woman from Colombia. They had a delightful love affair. Elisa had the wisdom to assemble a doctor team so that I could be the friend and confidant and not be responsible medically. This was a wise move on her part.

Such a quick march from full functioning to loss after loss was miserable, but fortunately David remained as kind and good humored as ever. One day he and I had a conversation that changed my life. As we were talking, he leaned over and spoke in a very intimate whisper:

"None of us gets out of here alive, John."

His words moved me unexpectedly. Perhaps our longtime friendship and many wonderful adventures together made his departure feel close to my own. I wear the persona of an accomplished doctor who has experience with the dying and a rich inner life. In reality, however, I am also fragile and fearful of my own mortality.

One night, some days before he died, we had the best lobster dinner anyone could imagine. David was a New England man through and through — reticent, strong, and reflective. His brother flew in from Maine with live lobsters — he had actually lost them at the airport in Philadelphia for a few hours, but finally managed to retrieve them. It was a wonderful evening. David was tired, weak, and sick, but he rose to the occasion, making toasts with fine wine to love and friendship.

A few days later, his brother and I sat with him. He had told Elisa that she should take her evening walk. His brother sat at the end of the bed, and I sat in a chair to the right of David's head. The room was quiet and peaceful. Quietly, so as not to disturb the peace, David's brother said, "I don't think he is breathing anymore." The doctor in me checked vital signs. It was so tranquil and gentle and, yes, he was gone.

Elisa soon returned. She intuitively knew David was gone. She knew her walk would take about six minutes as it was the same trajectory she took every evening around their apartment complex. She knew that this walk would be the time he would choose to depart because she also knew he didn't want her to be there when he finally left.

After David's death, I spoke to Elisa about her experience as a caregiver and she shared her insights with me. "The time between David's last appointment at the hospital and his death was very short. The doctor told him, "I have nothing more to offer you." Time really slowed down from that point on.

"The hospital orderlies helped load David into the car. The drive home was quiet. As I pulled up, I had no idea how I would get David out of the car, up three flights of stairs, and into his bed. Jane McGuire, a friend and nurse told me to call the fire department and get them to come help. I called them, crying. They were so sweet. They told me I didn't need to cry, and they arrived five minutes later.

"They were so gentle; they were like angels. They loaded him onto a stretcher and carried him up three flights of stairs and into bed. Our friend Tina was there at the time, and David gave her a big thumbs up, this was the way he needed to travel. They didn't cause him any pain.

"The fire captain called me over and asked one question. Did I know what I was going to do when David finally passed? I told him yes. I was emphatically clear. I was going to call my friend and doctor, John Horton. I only had one person to call. And John would take care of everything else. It gave me such peace of mind to have such a clear, simple plan.

"The day after the fire department carried him to his bed in our third-floor apartment, the big question was, what did David remember from that last appointment with the doctor? Together we reconstructed what was said. For the first few days, David was asking for extra treatment. It became a question of when he would accept the fact that there was nothing more.

"I felt no one needed to tell him, and I became like a dragon lady, protecting him from anyone who wanted to intellectualize it and spell it out. No one needed to tell him. He told us. He told me one day that he needed to let go and I needed to help him do that.

"Gradually, his speaking became harder to comprehend until no one could understand him but me. He developed hand signals to communicate with the hospice staff. By the time he passed, it had been several days since he'd spoken.

"In those days where time expanded, the house was always filled with people laughing and cooking. There were always chocolate chip cookies, David's favorite. There were many more than we could eat. We wound up with a freezer full of them. I was there for whatever David needed. I would ask him what he wanted for breakfast, and often it was more than he was able to eat. Toast, a smoothie, eggs. I would make it all and perhaps he would have a bite of this or that. After a while I began guiding his choices — like you might guide a child. No toast today, too scratchy on your throat.

"My brother is an ER doctor, and he and my friends were all waiting for me to crash after David died. It frightened me to consider meeting that expectation. I felt it was my duty to hold it together. In my grieving, I failed to see that I denied myself a gift of their love and support should I need to crash. It wasn't them judging me, it was their declaration — we want to help.

A few months later I was driving a friend to the airport and he asked me, "What is it like to live alone?" I was shocked. I didn't feel alone for one second. The love I shared with David continues and even grows."

Elisa did not crash and has not to this day, many years later. When I saw her a couple of months after David died, she told me, "Love overcomes fear." In the midst of this rapidly growing cancer that took him out in three short months, she made a very powerful strategic decision: her job was to love him, and she delegated everything else. She made sure that he was getting the best of care. She did a brilliant job.

That's a good strategy to support someone who is dying rapidly. Just choose to love them and let other people do all the other stuff. Professional caregivers are not able to provide love to the patient in the way that their most intimate partner can. This was an invaluable lesson for me. I have shared Elisa's words with many patients and caretakers with good results.

Later you will learn about the end of life home we created in Thousand Oaks that gave the families of dying people the kind of help that Elisa was able to create for David.

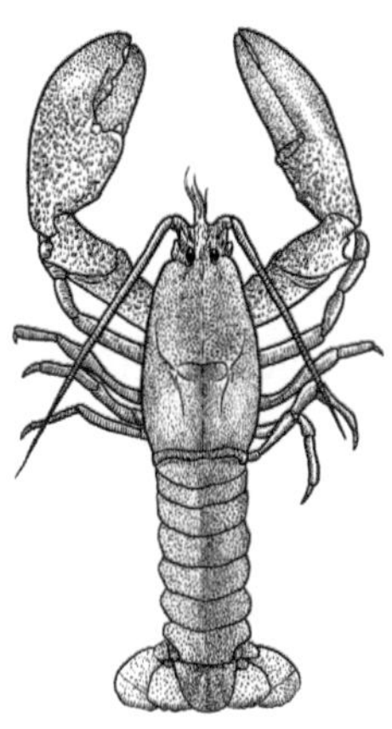

Love conquers fear.
—Elisa Cabal

11. El Jefe: Be the boss

EL JEFE WAS A DASHING FRANK SINATRA TYPE OF GUY in his late seventies. He had no fear of death and had aged well, like a good wine. He lived near my home, drove a red Corvette, and worked in public relations until the end. He had clocked over 45 years with top clients among the movers and shakers in Hollywood, in tourism for the government of Mexico, and for many splendid hotels and exotic travel destinations. Of course, El Jefe was not his real name, but this gentleman ran a tight ship, and a plaque with this title hung on his office wall. El Jefe means "the chief" or "the boss" in Spanish.

When it was El Jefe's turn to recognize that he had a fatal disease, he handled it as if he were piloting an airplane through very severe weather and heading for a safe landing — skillfully, entirely on his own terms. Because of my experience with him, I now have a very specific checklist of what can help make for a peaceful, graceful, departure.

El Jefe had mesothelioma, a dreadful, aggressive, treatment-resistant cancer that comes from exposure to asbestos. This exposure happened when he was a teenager working at the shipyards in Northern California. No one knew about the link between asbestos and cancer at that time, and it takes decades for this type of cancer to show up.

If people are diagnosed with mesothelioma fairly young, we cut out large amounts of the lung and give powerful chemotherapies with major side effects. It is a very uncomfortable and mostly futile treatment. El Jefe was too old for that.

But moreover, he was a California guy, a Mr. Natural, who had a reasonable wariness of the glitter of technological profit-driven California medicine. He looked to natural treatments such as nutritional supplements, exercise, and lots of chill time. At one point, he had checked into the hospital to have a minor procedure done so he could breathe better. He felt like a prisoner there; he had seen too many friends go to hospital for treatment and never return. He didn't want to do anything futile. He stated that no matter what he would never go to a hospital again. I did not argue with him about this and supported his explorations of natural treatments.

Although divorced, El Jefe maintained a caring relationship with his ex-wife and their children, and he enjoyed his social life. He lived by himself in a small, elegant house overlooking the lake of Westlake Village. I could walk from my house to his along a green belt path by the lake. This was convenient as he became increasingly disabled.

My first meeting with him in my office was memorable. His daughter introduced him to me as a possible doctor. She knew her father as El Jefe and that he would not tolerate being in an inferior position with anyone, including a doctor. I explained my position, which is that a doctor-patient relationship is, in the main, an equal partnership. The doctor knows more about medicine than the patient does, while the patient knows more about themselves than the doctor does. With humor, I added that — as he well knew from years in business — at some point one partner emerges as the senior partner for good or bad reasons. Then I asked him, in this relationship whom he thought would become the senior partner? He paused as all patients do when asked this question. I told him that the senior partner would always be him. A doctor is hired help and can be fired for any cause. This satisfied him and a bond of mutual respect and humorous rapport evolved over a few good years before the mesothelioma showed up.

El Jefe referred to death as the next new adventure, and his initial diagnosis didn't faze him. His approach was to try any nutritional idea that appealed to him. As the disease began to overtake him, it was hard for him to get up and move around. Bodily functions were becoming problematic. One day I could see he was very uncomfortable.

"So, what's the good news, Doc?"

He was always ready for some good news.

I didn't try to sugarcoat it. I informed him that we would need to bring him a hospital bed and hospice nurses to care for him at home until his daughter could come. He didn't want anyone caring for him in his home, but that is not unusual among the proudly independent elders in Southern California — we still want to drive a car when we can barely walk or see.

With a calm, seasoned look in his eyes, he understood that there was nothing more we could do to make him better. It felt surreal, and it was sad, yet somehow it was a release. The end of his illness and disability was near. There was nothing more I could say to him at that moment. He knew I would be there for him and help him get what he needed. His next "new adventure" was on the horizon.

That was a magical moment for me. He already accepted his deadly diagnosis. Now the point of no return was palpable. My image then was that we were in an airplane flying with one engine rather than two. The pilot had told us that he can land the plane safely with the one engine that had not failed. Shortly after that announcement we see the working engine explode and the plane starts to fall out the sky. It was like that as El Jefe and I understood that now he was falling.

The morning after our conversation, he fell on his way to the bathroom and was unable to get up. So that very day, the hospital bed arrived, along with my favorite hospice nurse to bring the next level of care to him in his home. She knew exactly how to step in.

His daughter soon arrived from overseas and began rearranging his furniture. Always good in a crisis, El Jefe took it all in stride and good humor. He began the process of radical acceptance. His world was collapsing around him as his numerous mementos were cleared aside to make way for the hospital bed. He was keenly aware that he was entering a new threshold.

His daughter purchased a sleeping bag so that she could sleep on the couch by his hospital bed. A few days later, she called me to come by one evening. He wasn't breathing well. One lung had been filled with cancer for some time. As I listened to the other lung, very little air was moving. It was filling with fluid or an infection. In either case, it meant that he was fading more quickly. He was fully conscious and not in any distress, just not breathing well. I told him I didn't think he would last more than a day or two unless he went to the hospital. He was clear: no hospital.

Ironically, earlier that day when asked to sign a Do Not Resuscitate order, he refused. Agreeing to a DNR is usually a requirement when switching to hospice care for the elderly. He told the hospice team that if his heart stopped, they should get it going again; but he wouldn't go to the hospital. Savoring the last days of life, he did not want to die of an easily reversible cardiac event. The hospice nurse and I figured it was okay in this situation because even if paramedics came to the house, we would not allow them to take him to the hospital, as per El Jefe's request. This was a first for the experienced hospice nurse — in her many years of hospice nursing no one had ever refused to sign a DNR. El Jefe was leaving on his own terms, still savoring his life at home with his daughter. This wine was good to the last swallow.

That evening, El Jefe was having more difficulty breathing but was not in distress or pain. I examined his lungs again and told him that I did not think he would last the night without medical care in a hospital. He took this in without comment and continued to enjoy channel-surfing the TV at the foot of his bed.

His daughter and I went to the kitchen to talk about this new development — his second lung now failing him. Heart failure or pneumonia would be easy to treat and reverse in a day or two in hospital. We seriously considered calling the paramedics — maybe they could convince him to go to the hospital. But we knew that would be a disaster; he would surely kick them out and be upset with us. I remembered the first rule of medicine: first do no harm. We think of harm as physical, but it is also psychological. Calling the paramedics might have given us peace of mind, but it would have harmed him. At a certain point, trying to fix someone rather than letting them be becomes a form of aggression.

El Jefe was not outwardly anxious at all, we were the ones who were anxious. He didn't need to make any compromises. We were simply not ready for him to leave yet. We regrouped and went back to sit with him. At one point he said, "I want to get up."

His daughter was visibly concerned; he was six feet tall and could easily fall out of bed if he tried to stand up, let alone walk. She wondered if he remembered that he could no longer walk.

I understood that he wanted to check again to see if his legs could still carry him, and I helped him try. As his feet rested on the ground with me supporting his back, he realized that he could not possibly stand. The strength to stand had left him. He inched closer to his departure time. It was as if the three of us were watching a countdown to takeoff.

The anticipation was not painful or even suspenseful. With his one working lung filling with infection and fluid it was certain that his life would soon end. He simply lay back. I managed to turn him properly, so he was as comfortable as possible. He mostly channel surfed and occasionally looked at us with a reassuring look in his eyes: I'm okay, you guys can relax.

It was around 9:00 pm when I left. I walked home by the light of the moon thinking of this noble man winding down in the peace of his home. I felt that if one can ever say that dying is beautiful, this might just be the time. As I cruised along, I was singing/chanting to myself over and over again — hero, hero, hero, gone, gone, gone.

After I left, his daughter sat with him quietly, feeling content and easy within herself. She told me later that she intuitively knew he was very busy in his process. Occasionally she wondered if there was more to say, or some way to help. As a father and daughter, they had always been close, so words were not necessary. The advice from a friend echoed inside her: You don't have to "do" anything. Just be there.

At 7:00 a.m. his daughter called me. "I think he is gone." "You think?" I asked ironically with kindness. She said, "Yes, he is dead."

When I walked in, he was lying perpendicular across the hospital bed. As his daughter lay sleeping, he evidently had tried to get up again. Somehow this did not surprise me. He was an independent man of action and hope — why not give standing on his own two legs another try? In a way he did, he rose and departed on to the next new adventure.

There was a palpable peace in the air, and his daughter and I looked at one another, sad but not disturbed. Soon his other daughter arrived with her children and eventually the whole family. Everyone was sad but also in awe, it was smooth sailing for El Jefe. He did it his way until the very end. It was a fine and graceful departure.

12. Eva: Knowing what you need

EVA WAS CREATIVE AND SOCIAL—AN UNUSUAL COMbination in my experience. She had an unwavering momentum of life that was impressive for someone of her age. She grew up in Vienna, then moved to America, became a well-known artist, married a successful doctor, had a family, lived in New York City, and then retired to Ojai, California. She was clearly a force in the world and a woman in control.

Late on a Friday afternoon, I received an emergency call from Eva's gastroenterologist who felt a large mass in her abdomen. He thought it was probably a cancer obstructing the colon. Eva had requested that I be involved with her care, which surprised me as I had only seen her a few times for minor problems. Before we even had a diagnosis, the specialist was talking about hospice care. She refused.

At the colonoscopy, her doctor found a very large mass representing a chronic inflammation of the colon. It was a huge relief that she did not have a deadly advanced colon cancer. In her few weeks of hospital care and recovery, I came to know and enjoy this delightful woman and to gain some insight into how this mass might have developed.

When she was 10 years old, Eva and some of her family escaped from Vienna, shortly after Hitler invaded. She was from a wealthy Jewish family that had deep cultural roots in Austria. She experienced the gradual discrimination and then exclusion of Jews from everyday life in Vienna. Then came deportations and the rumors of concentration and death camps. Her family had the means to escape and eventually she landed in New York City. Any of her family members who remained in Vienna were murdered one way or another by the Nazis.

Eva had another trauma that may have been part of this intestinal inflammation. This was the murder of her eldest son and his wife — a senseless act of violence, a random robbery and killing in their home in Arizona. In the aftermath of this devastating tragedy, Eva provided love and support to her granddaughter, her second son, and various other relatives. She was the rock for the family. I could only imagine how traumatized she was by the murder, which had to have triggered painful memories of the Holocaust.

Perhaps holding everything together as she did with such courage and dignity led to this intestinal inflammation. The gastrointestinal system is very much connected to emotion. Think of the common phrases: a gut-wrenching experience, keeping your shit together, verbal diarrhea, constipation of emotional expression, to poop your pants from fear, the nausea of the meaningless — all of these phrases express the connection between our gut and our emotions. We know that serotonin in the brain has to do with mood, yet there is more serotonin in the large intestine than there is in the brain. So, we can label our digestive system as our instinctual brain.

Eva did well after hospitalization, except that she developed fluctuating high blood pressure. This is a common situation, especially in the elderly. Eva had busy productive days and bouts of high blood pressure at night. The medications caused unwanted side effects, so it was difficult to make sure that her blood pressure was neither too high nor too low. I suspected that the blood pressure elevations at night had something to do with the painful losses she had experienced and her fears, growing up in the shadow of the Holocaust. These pains and fears were deep within her and we could never find a way to process or resolve them.

Over time, she became more tired and vulnerable. Finally, we admitted her to the hospital for a thorough evaluation, but the testing and studies did not show any treatable disease. Eva did not like the hospital; it was stressful for her rather than restful. She wanted her remaining time to be under her control.

The neurology consultant was sure he could find a disease of the brain that we could treat to revive her life. Eva knew enough to be reasonably suspicious of the neurologist going on a fishing expedition, doing whatever it took to find something to treat, whether it would help or not. None of her family or the other doctors wanted to submit her to more testing but as happens in these situations, we went along with it until she firmly refused an invasive test, a spinal tap.

Neither the family nor I could see her living happily anywhere but in her peaceful, art-filled home. But then, in the midst of this nightmare, she had a massive stroke that destroyed 25 percent of her brain. Before we could object, the aggressive neurologist had her intubated and put in intensive care. Suddenly a machine was breathing for her, and her blood pressure was fully regulated with multiple IV lines. Everything was regulated to keep her alive indefinitely. Everything was being done TO her, without her consent.

For a few days, her son, Jeff, conducted intensive, long distance family conferences to decide what to do. The decision was simple enough. Either withdraw the life support and see if she could live and heal without it, or keep her on life support indefinitely and watch her body deteriorate gradually from lack of movement.

My counsel was simple. She was fading before the massive stroke, so even if she recovered enough to come off life support, her deficit would be much greater. No more painting, no more cooking a Sunday Austrian lunch for friends (including me), no more visits back to Ojai for walks in the mountains, and perhaps no more coherent thinking or talking.

The neurologist and the intensive care unit doctors did not want to be part of the discussion. Predictably they hid in the technical challenges of ICU care. It was just me and Jeff considering the big picture. Soon it was decided, a clear go ahead from the family, let's pull the plug. I was relieved. So there we are, Jeff and I, at the ICU to do just that. A doctor I did not know was examining Eva when we arrived. I explained what Jeff had decided with my counsel; that he had medical power of attorney and her advanced directive had explicitly said no intubation or intensive care. He asked us to wait until he finished his infectious disease consult. We waited, talking about this request. What was the value of his consult now that she was going to die? Perhaps he wanted to finish so he could get paid. It was bizarre.

Eva lived for a few peaceful minutes after life support was withdrawn. Her quiet, slow breathing felt like a blessed release from the tyranny of the machines. Then she exhaled a last slow breath which was not followed by an inhale. We were sad but also grateful that she was free from future medical suffering.

One of Eva's paintings hangs in my office. I remember her not only for the preciousness of her friendship but also for her introducing me to Dr. Eric Kendal, the Nobel Prize-winning doctor who wrote the book, *In Search of Memory: The Emergence of a New Science of the Mind.* Eva and Dr. Kendal had been children together in Vienna before Hitler invaded Austria. His family escaped as hers did and they knew one another in New York City before she moved to California.

Speaking at Eva's memorial I was grateful to express my appreciation for the love and learning I had experienced as her doctor and friend over all those good years. The occasion also relieved me of any lingering concern that I had perhaps not done enough to help her get healthy and stay alive for a longer time. I knew that her family had appreciated that she reached her shelf life and could leave peacefully without the ordeal of subjecting her to futile medicine.

■ ■ ■

As a personal aside, knowing Eva impacted my own life when she took me to meet Doctor Kendal at the premiere of a film about him at the Skirball Cultural Center in Los Angeles. In his talk that afternoon, he mentioned casually that the Jews of Europe and America had not yet healed from the PTSD of the Holocaust. This simple statement from the Nobel laureate doctor hit a deep, raw current of pain and sadness in my being.

I understood in that moment the puzzle of my father's profound emotional and mental problems. I understood that he had changed his family name from Horowitz to Horton to protect his children from bias and prejudice. I never understood until then that the steel that surrounded his heart was the trans-generational PTSD of the Holocaust. Years of my own psychotherapy as well as my own practice of counseling in the context of general medicine had never made clear this source of suffering. That we mirror the inner lives of our parents is true. That we can be unaware of a hidden source of pain in parents and even society in general is also true.

13. Officer Higgins: The choice to end it

OUR HOSPICE CARE TEAM HAD WEEKLY CONVERSATIONS about each patient. For the most part, these were routine follow-ups about known and stable patients. Problems were usually taken care of and resolved by the next weekly meeting, but there was one patient who we discussed at each meeting over a number of weeks. Officer Higgins was a retired policeman in his fifties, who had enjoyed excellent health and was known as a kind and understanding policeman before a catastrophic cancer took hold of him. His untreatable head and neck cancer had left the man disfigured; he was disgusted with his appearance.

The man and his wife were the managers of the small apartment complex where they lived. His wife had arranged his hospital bed in their dining room next to the kitchen where there was also a small shop for people who lived in the complex to pick up basics like milk, bread, and coffee.

She'd placed his bed there so that he would interact with the few people who might come into the shop. But he hated this exposure to people and made it clear that he wanted to spend time with his son — who lived outside of Las Vegas — and to die away from the watching eyes of people coming and going. His wife fought him on this because she was not ready for him to retreat and die away from their home. The hospice staff were frustrated by this battle.

Even though he was medically stable, the nursing and social work team asked me to see him to help settle the tug of war. The small apartment was a bizarre scene with the hospital bed crammed into the dining room bordering the small eat-in family kitchen and little shop. No walls or even screens separated these areas.

So, he was on display, with the ugly cancer growing in his neck, his vulnerability and helplessness plain for all to see. It was like a scene from a horror movie. We had a conversation about his deep longing to go to his son's home where he could rest, not be force fed, and could gently leave in peace. He had a rather regal bearing as a strong police officer with an ironic sense of his mortality. We had a good time together sharing vintage Italian jokes from his happier days and my childhood. His wife observed us from a distance, not with pleasure. Perhaps she thought us foolish to laugh in the face of his demise. She wouldn't budge in her refusal to let him go his way.

Then one day he shot himself in the head with a revolver. His wife was completely horrified. The hospice nurses were sad but not surprised.

Some months later, we had another patient with a similar inoperable disfiguring neck cancer. He was found by his family with a revolver. they stopped him from pulling the trigger. I went to consult. He told me he didn't want to live the way he was. He was disgusted by the mass growing and disfiguring his neck and face. His pain was controlled but he had no pleasure and certainly no hope for anything better. He just wanted to die.

There is no problem with going gently into the night, so I suggested he could stop eating and drinking. He liked that idea. I asked the family how they felt about it and if it was a problem for them. They did not like the idea, but they accepted his choice easily once they really listened to him. I assured him that as he became weak and his body shut down, we would not put in a feeding tube to keep him alive. For a few days, not eating was a little uncomfortable, but his body adapted. It took about two weeks for him to go gently into the night. In contrast to Officer Higgins, he did it his way. The result was a peaceful departure that family and friends could appreciate.

We had another patient, a psychologist, who planned her departure carefully. She collected lots of different medications, set a date to take them, had friends over that evening to say goodbye, took the meds, and lay down in bed in the arms of her daughter to sleep her way into death.

She woke up in the morning with a hangover from all the meds, disappointed but surprisingly calm. In her calm, she understood that she had not created her life so perhaps it was not her right to destroy it. When I went to see her in her comfortable, well-furnished, elegant home, she was enjoying a richer inner life and had decided she could live out her days in the shadow of dying.

14. Hospice: Doing it your way

RELATIVE TO THE SUICIDE STORIES I JUST TOLD, I AM always asked about whether doctor-assisted suicide is an answer to those suffering in pain. Doctor William Lamers, my mentor in learning hospice medicine, invited me to be co-director of a home hospice in the San Fernando Valley. He was part of the creation of the modern hospice movement in England with Dame Sicely Saunders. In all of Dr. Lamers's decades of hospice doctoring, teaching, and leadership, he only found a handful of patients who could not be helped out of their depression, pain, frustration, or anger in dying. Certainly, this requires a quality of medical care that may not be available to everyone. However, for any individual, there is an inner process that has integrity, dignity, hope, and clarity.

Doctor Lamers once chaired a discussion of doctor-assisted suicide at the Malibu Medical Society meeting one fine summer evening. It was a dramatic event where many people shared strong opinions. At that time, there was a case being debated in Los

Angeles. A young woman severely injured in a car accident had been in a semi-comatose state, on life support, in a nursing home for years. The parents wanted to disconnect her and let nature take its course. The doctors and clergy involved did not want to risk her life by withdrawing the modest life support. Do we preserve this life indefinitely or release her from a meaningless existence? It was an extreme situation — especially because she was not able to make a conscious request herself.

Lamers' wisdom was evident in the discussion of options. The humanistic perspective, apart from medical legal concerns for the doctors, family quarrels, and finances, supported feeling. Feeling is a way of knowing. When Lamers brought the conversation around to feeling, we took some time to reflect. No one wanted to keep this woman in limbo. Best to remove life support and see if the life force gets her up or she dies peacefully. For those who are misinformed, they may believe the purpose of hospice is to speed up the death process.

Requests to end the agony of dying are not infrequent. From his vast experience, Doctor Lamers made it clear that these requests occur because a person is afraid or in pain or frustrated in some way. He estimated that in his experience, in 99 out of 100 cases, with good medicine and wise psychological and social support, these issues can be addressed and resolved in a way that allows the person to enjoy their last days.

In those last days, it can be time for framing the possibility of coming back to those qualities we were born with, allowing us to create the vision and preparations for the end of life. This is a time to nurture the seeds of hope and inner peace.

Hospice is about finding a safe and supported space where you have all the time you need, in due process, to depart. This time can be a gift that we can socially provide to one another, if we choose to see the need. Practitioners of ancient Greek medicine understood this and provided places for this to happen. In Dr. Michael Kearney's introduction to his book, *A Place of Healing: Working with Nature and Soul at the End,* written mainly for caregivers of dying people, he states:

> "In ancient Greece at the very beginning of western healthcare, we find two intertwined systems of early scientific medicine, derived from the teachings of the great physician Hippocrates, and a form of psychological and spiritual healing based on the ritual practice of Asklepios, the Greek god of healing. Whereas Hippocratic medicine, representing the beginnings of the medical model concentrated on the treatment of curable conditions, Asklepion healing was primarily concerned with helping those suffering from incurable conditions. Where Hippocratic practice emphasized the need for a rational and evidence-based approach and was dependent on an external agent to achieve its effect, the Asklepion rites assumed that there was a spontaneous tendency towards wholeness within each individual and healing came through cooperation with this inner dynamic. Here was a culture that recognized the value of two fundamentally different but complementary models of care. Here was an integrated system of healthcare which attended to patients as whole persons: body, mind, soul, and spirit."

15. Igor: Telling your loved one it is okay for them to go

LATE ONE FRIDAY, I WALKED INTO A SMALL APARTMENT in a poor neighborhood in the San Fernando Valley. The patient's wife and middle-aged son sat at the small kitchen table, looking overwhelmed. They began telling me how difficult things were. The dying man was so weak that he had not left his bed for days. He barely ate and was mostly unconscious. There was very little left of him and no hope for medical improvement, but somehow, he had a tenacious will to live. For weeks, he had been holding on without a shred of a hope of getting better. He was not at peace, nor was he responsive to family and friends; he was anxious and uncomfortable. The whole situation felt wrong, but no doctor wanted to sedate and kill him. Everyone was exhausted, including the hospice staff. This is why I had been asked to do an emergency visit on a Friday evening. I was curious as to why he was holding on, so I asked. In doing so, I uncovered a family secret.

With difficulty and courage, the mother told her son about her experience with a severe mental illness that had required hospitalizations when he and his sister were young. Her husband kept this knowledge from the children and, with great effort, protected his wife from stress. As she was explaining to her son how hard his father had worked to hide her illness, some things about the family dynamics started making sense. Mother and son called the estranged sister and the epiphany of revelations and understanding continued. It was a surprising and most welcome conversation. I felt a bit of an intruder, a catalyst but not a participant. I excused myself to visit the man of the hour.

I entered the bedroom and before me was a region of hell that Dante didn't describe. There was hardly any life left in this man who had given so much to keep his family together. I understood when I saw him why the hospice people had asked me to see him. He was skin and bones, shaking all over, and so uncomfortable. I felt that he could not leave because he was still holding them together. His wife did not want him to be sedated with painkillers because, as I now understood, she knew he wanted to be conscious — a really difficult position for the hospice staff.

I didn't know where his consciousness was, but I stood at the foot of the bed and spoke to him as if he were fully there. I explained everything to him, just as I would have if he were a new patient:

> "This is what's wrong with you. There is nothing to be done, your body is worn out. I have been talking to your family and they understand you've been holding on to protect your wife. They are grateful for your efforts all these years. It seems you've been holding on for a long time. Now is the time, if you can, to leave, to let go of holding the

> family together. Mission accomplished: you can leave in a heroic peace. Please do so, as it will be a relief for everyone including you."

I was inspired from the kitchen love fest and my words felt true and timely. He didn't respond to my kind words.

I told the family what I had said to their dear husband and father about their revelation and epiphany. It was kind of a religious experience that was happening around that kitchen table late on that cold Friday evening — quite different from the dismal scene in the bedroom.

A week later, I went to the usual hospice meeting and the nurse who was involved with this family told me he had died the night of our conversation. He had passed away with his wife holding him, thanking him, and telling him everything was okay and that he could go. That was a whole lot better than knocking him out with some kind of medicine when he was still not okay psychologically.

A well-known principle of hospice medicine is that family and friends need to give a dying person permission to let go and move on. This is an expression of love and understanding. We do not want to see a person suffer because we are not ready for them to leave. We need to assure them that we will be okay. This can be the most intimate expression of kindness we can give to a dying person. Permission to leave is also a statement of trust. Trust in the nature of life and death, trust in the person leaving, and trust in ourselves. Trust that we will be okay, that we can grieve and stay sane, and our life will continue to evolve after they are gone.

Where there is ruin
there is hope for treasure.
–Rumi

UNDERSTANDING 3

Embrace Simplicity

THE COMPLEXITY OF THE HUMAN BODY IS BEYOND comprehension. However, each bodily system has a simple purpose. The heart circulates the blood, the immune system kills invasive germs, the digestive system converts food to energy, and so on and on it goes. At birth as at death, it is the breath that is the key. It carries the life force. This is simple.

As death approaches, we can embrace the breath and enjoy the simple company of the life force. From this place, an awareness of a death without fear is obvious. It is the same as the lack of fear a toddler feels in learning to walk. They embrace the possibility unendingly. Simplicity can be like that. Trusting the goodness of existence is not complicated. Certainly, there are the fears of despair, the unknown, pain and punishment, but the simple goodness of existence is more attractive and can carry us through.

Our common needs in those days are basic: safety, comfort, and peace — safe from aggressive medicine, comfortable physically, emotionally, and mentally in the company of good caretakers (not always so easy to get) and free to uncover the peace within. If we are clear about these needs and the other understandings, we can actually bring out the best in caretakers. A grateful kind heart connects to the same in others. There have always been those patients that all the staff enjoy being with during the day or night. Encouraging and being encouraged can come from the person being taken care of as well as the caretakers.

Our brains allow us to adapt to all kinds of situations. Our ideas and concepts mostly come from our families, cultures, and friends. We live in the goals we are given and accept. We judge our successes based on whether we achieve these goals. Our brain can also become simpler as our social lives are less demanding or as we are approaching departure. The needs of the heart can become more clear.

What is in our adaptive brains is relative to what our life has become over many years. What is in our hearts is from the DNA of human consciousness. Is the ability to feel peace, love, and joy part of our DNA? I think yes, emphatically. This is the essence of the human being. Just as dolphins love to play and jump in the water, humans love to feel love and joy. The current of wisdom across all cultures points to these qualities of experience as being the essence of the human being. I say it is in our DNA because it is seen across all cultures and all time. Tiny babies have the ability to feel contentment, peace, serenity, joy. Why not a departing person as well?

The biggest block to feeling the simplicity of existence is that we have a hard time accepting all the love that exists for us for no reason.

16. The power of touch

IN MY BETHESDA PRACTICE, THERE WAS AN ELDERLY man who would come in for a visit every few months. He had a litany of aches, pains, concerns, and an occasional serious-sounding symptom. I would take my time giving him a full physical examination while asking about his life and listening carefully. He was popular in our office because every time I gave him a good bill of health, he would loudly announce to the patients in the waiting room that I had healed him from all his ills. He was serious and it was true. He just needed some talking and physical contact. I didn't know that at the time.

■ ■ ■

"I was afraid to touch her." Nora was afraid of her mother's fragility and was repulsed by her appearance. It was only when her mother finally passed that Nora reached out and touched her. She discovered that her mother's hair and skin were baby soft, and her tears flowed as she realized her mistake.

We hold a newborn infant close, yet we often fear touching the elderly. An elderly person is not necessarily more fragile than a newborn. The benefits of touch are the same for both. Touch is a communication that transcends age, time, and language. Even before we open our eyes or take our first breath, gentle touch releases oxytocin which calms us and lets us know someone cares. We have less oxytocin as we age, but a simple thing like touch helps release it, no matter our age. While some people are averse to it because of a bad experience in their life, we can hold the dying by touching and massaging their hands and feet, and we can hold the dying with our presence, our words, or our sense of quiet.

Because Sushila had her third child while helping me write this book, I took a chance to revisit an important book from my early doctoring days. The book, called *Birth Without Violence* published in 1974, was a revelation for young doctors interested in the humanization of medicine. Here is an edited expression from the publisher of a revised edition:

> *Birth Without Violence is the first book to express what mothers have always known, babies are born complete human beings with the ability to experience a full range of human emotions. First published in 1974, it revolutionized the way we perceive the process of birth urging us to see it from the infant's point of view. Why must a child emerge from the quiet darkness of the womb into a blaze of blinding light and loud voices? Think of a hospital Intensive Care Unit with lots of machine noise. Why must an infant take its first*

breathing terror hanging upside down as its vulnerable spine is jerked straight? Why must the infant be separated from its mother after spending nine months in her nourishing body?

I remember being at births that appreciated the needs of the infant to be born in the kinder environment of a birth center or birthing room rather than in the operating room. It reminds a me of the difference between the death I saw back in India that helped me recover from the pain of extreme deaths at San Francisco General Hospital.

What about in dying? People who are overly medicated at the end are often said to have been killed by the pain medications. Numbed out. Medications can certainly numb the senses and even hasten death. Perhaps people dying with no or minimal medication are more able to access this same feel-good hormone. Touch helps a person produce oxytocin, bringing them a natural toolkit to carry them through pain. In this way, we can help relieve a person's pain and minimize the risk of overmedicating.

Here is a letter to *The New York Times* written in response to a well-read op-ed piece that discussed end-of-life directives. The point of the op-ed piece was that end-of-life directives can be flexible, depending upon changing conditions and attitudes. This touching letter supports the view that just holding hands provides more relief than morphine.

My dad was one of those people who changed their minds about end-of-life care. Before getting cancer, he thought his top priority when suffering would be to get lots of morphine. When he was actually dying, he discovered that he hated morphine. It made him extremely constipated, gave him disturbing hallucinations, and impaired his ability to be conscious and kind in his final days.

His health care proxy came by every day and turned up the morphine, and my dad always turned it down. He said he did not have that much pain. If he lay still, he found that he got more relief from holding hands.

— Anne Barschall

There was another opinion piece in *The New York Times* not long ago by a psychologist who said that she would like to be snowed with morphine in her last days. Her attitude was — no drama or trauma, just a morphine drip. I was amazed. Didn't she know that there are serious side effects to such a strategy like intense constipation, scary hallucinations, less effectiveness over time, and then more pain? Not that pain killers are not helpful, but to sacrifice the choice of being conscious and the ability to learn — even in our last hours — is a big mistake. The idea of going out, literally, in a drug-induced coma is as seductive as it is foolish. Morphine and other pain medications are of wonderful benefit but require skillful decision making to ensure the best supportive outcome.

17. Two questions before considering extreme measures

THERE IS NO MAGICAL HEALING IN THE ICU. THE ICU is really tough on the body, especially for the elderly. The brilliance of advanced medicine can save the lives of people who still have some good years left. I love to see that. I am referring to what we call futile medicine which is keeping people alive in advanced old age with critical illness, who even if they survive the ICU will not have a quality of life they would find acceptable. It is a wrenching experience for family as well to witness the patient undergoing futile medicine in the hospital ICU.

In a required weekend training for physicians at my hospital in Southern California, a professor of philosophy and ethics taught us how to choose whether or not to put a critically ill elderly patient into intensive care. He taught the course with a lawyer, and they noted how this is a very tough decision for any medical team. There is usually not a lot of time to deliberate the pros and cons and there is an extensive menu of technical concerns and possibilities. Will time in intensive care cure a serious illness in an old person? Will it be possible to take this person off intensive care soon? How will the patient and family feel about this extreme treatment? There are many more purely medical concerns.

The doctor and lawyer had done extensive research on these issues at a large Los Angeles hospital. They found that gathering the family of the patient before beginning ICU treatment and asking just two questions was all that was needed to make the decision.

The first question was whether the patient was enjoying everyday life and looking forward to good things in the future like anniversaries, graduations, vacations, etc. or was the person talking about being done with life and wanting to leave.

The second question was what would the person say if they were conscious about being put into the ICU. The caveat is that when someone goes into ICU treatment, if they survive, their quality of life will be worse.

In short, they found that in under ten minutes, there was unanimous clarity among the family regarding whether the elderly patient entering the ICU was a Yes or a No.

18. Hospice can keep it simple

WE NEED TO UNDERSTAND HOSPICE, AS MANY PEOPLE are deathly afraid of hospice. I admit that I once held a commonly believed, completely uninformed view of hospice that when a patient enters hospice care, everyone would really prefer that the person die sooner rather than later. My belief was a fear shared by many patients and families who receive word that their loved one has entered hospice. Actually, hospice is an opportunity to slow down. Hospice gets paid for taking care of patients when active treatments are no longer being pursued. The cousin of hospice, palliative care, focuses solely on comfort, and not aggressive treatments. Studies have shown that patients live longer in a palliative care and hospice environment as compared to active treatments for terminal illness. Of course, this is statistical, and each situation is different. There is always the dynamic relationship between the science and art of medicine.

When I first began to practice in Westlake Village, Dr. William Lamers invited me to be his assistant medical director at an outpatient hospice near my general practice. I was cautious about this invitation, because I had little knowledge of hospice then, and I did not think that dealing with dying patients would be rewarding. After all, we doctors do what we do to cure or slow down illness, not to watch people die. I was to be pleasantly surprised to learn how much can be done to relieve suffering, making things better and being helpful right up to the last breaths.

Dr. Lamers was a burly, bear-like man with a blend of British humor, keen medical skills, empathy, and warmth. He had worked closely with Dame Cicely Saunders, the brave nurse who started the modern Western hospice movement in 1967 in England. He generated a sense of well-being in the most difficult situations. His confidence that no patient would ever need to live in unbearable pain was based on vast experience, wisdom, and a stubborn will.

Every week, Dr. Lamers and I would conduct a clinical review of the ongoing care of each of the 20 or 30 patients in the outpatient hospice with the nurses, social workers, administrators, and clergy. Occasionally they would dispatch me to the home of a patient for a consult. All of our patients had medical doctors, but we were the ones to fine-tune their hospice care.

People often fear pain at the end. But pain doesn't have to be an issue. Dame Cicely Saunders argued that pain exists in four dimensions; physical, social, psychological, and spiritual. She understood and taught that all four types of pain can be treated and resolved. Her work is totally applicable today. She named her hospice after Saint Christopher because he is the patron saint of travelers. She saw death as our last adventure.

Another way of looking at pain is to see that it initially has value, telling us something is wrong that needs attention. If what is wrong is evident and we have a clear plan to fix it, the pain diminishes. The body is not stupid. However, if we do not understand the pain, fear creeps in. Could it be a serious, untreatable condition?

If we don't address the fear, then here comes anxiety with many faces. If this confusion, fear, and anxiety go on for some time, we can end up in the dungeon of helplessness and hopelessness. All this is preventable if we apply Dame Cecily Saunders's wisdom.

Remember pain is the body telling us something is wrong. That's very valuable. If you get up at night and stub your toe, it might hurt badly. You take a look, and if it's not broken or bleeding you get back into bed and the pain goes away. Now if you wake up with abdominal pain, you might think, well, I ate late, so I'm a little gassy. But then comes the fear that you could have appendicitis. The pain becomes stronger when you're caught in the fear of appendicitis. If you don't resolve that fear of appendicitis, here comes anxiety.

Anxiety has a hundred faces. Fear is very specific: I fear I have appendicitis. If I dismiss that fear, it's just like the stubbed toe, I don't get caught up in the pain. Fear needs to be defined and redefined until whatever it is simply becomes a challenge and you're no longer afraid. We can accept, face, and resolve challenges no matter what they are. Unnecessary fear is just that, unnecessary.

In hospice when we successfully address the fear, anxiety, blame, or guilt of a person, treating the causes of the physical pain is not difficult. I have had many end-of-life adventures as the hospice's trouble-shooting doctor. These encounters with dying patients were brief and sometimes remarkably profound. In these encounters, I learned the principles of hospice medical care.

In a recent conversation with an elderly patient who wanted me to advise him about physician-assisted suicide in the face of a terminal illness, I asked him which of the multiple heads of the dragon of death scared him. What alarmed him, he said, was the possibility of unbearable pain. I told him with great certainty that good pain control is possible with the right personal understanding and skillful medical treatment. I assure you my twenty years of hospice experience plus the lessons from everyday medicine back up my radical claim.

19. Ingrid: Death without violence

INGRID WAS THE HANDSOME, COMPETENT LADY BEHIND the counter at the gem of a European bakery where I had my morning coffee and a muffin near my office. She was a compact woman with a soft German accent. Everyone loved that bakery where Ingrid was the welcoming person who provided the human warmth as well as the wonderful coffee and delectable pastries first thing in the morning.

Ingrid's reflections of her childhood in Germany were highlighted by memories of bombs and the allied soldiers who stormed the city and raped the women. She had profound post-traumatic stress, but it wasn't obvious. Her personality was a curious blend of toughness and a tender vulnerability. Her trauma had happened when she was very young and it was so impersonal that she had no bitterness or resentment toward people.

Eventually, Ingrid's bakery was closed to make way for a Blockbuster Video store. I missed my mornings with her. She reappeared as the hostess of a nearby upscale restaurant. The first time we met again at that restaurant, she asked if I would be her doctor. I was delighted by her trust in me, but I did not know then how ill she had been for some time. She appeared as a strong self-sufficient woman doing well in her sixties; however Ingrid had severe diabetes and chose not to do much about it. People loved her, but her post-traumatic stress caused her to shut down and she would sometimes collapse for months. As I cared for her, it was clear that at some point her health was going to give out. She would reach her shelf life sooner rather than later as a result of early childhood trauma.

The day came when Ingrid could no longer be cared for at home; her boyfriend had become exhausted trying to care for her in their small home. Her daughter was now in charge and over the first few days in hospital, I understood that Ingrid had not been happy for quite a while. We hoped that getting her diabetes in control would improve her life, but perhaps not. She seemed to be running out of steam as do even the best German trains.

I got a call on my cell phone from Ingrid's daughter asking me to talk with the hospital doctor. She was having a stroke in the hospital right there in real time. The hospital doctor wanted to transfer her to intensive care where she would be intubated and put on mechanical life support with a number of IVs and medications.

The aggressiveness of medicine is attractive. Yes, we can take care of this. Yes, we can keep your mother alive for a while longer. Yes, we have a procedure. Yes, we have some medicine. It's all designed to preserve life at any cost, ignoring the psychological and social implications of the treatment. This is cover-your-ass and profit-based medicine at its worst.

Human wisdom is indispensable to good medicine, but many doctors feel we do not have the time to have a real dialogue with patients or family, and there are no insurance codes to bill and be paid for the time spent attempting to help bring wisdom into the decision making.

Fortunately, Ingrid's daughter had my cell phone and she called me before all that "good stuff" came down on her mom.

"Hi, this is Doctor Horton, how is Ingrid?"

"She is having a massive stroke and going into a coma," the hospital doctor said. "We must move her to intensive care immediately. Her vital signs are poor."

"No. Let's not do that. Please simply let her be. If she dies now, it will be okay. Neither Ingrid nor her daughter nor I as her doctor want intensive care at this time in her life," I said.

"She is in the hospital, and we must take her to intensive care now," he said.

"I know that is your instinctive medical response, but she has an end-of-life care document in her chart that precludes intensive-care life support. You are being instructed by her personal doctor and her daughter not to do this as it is not the wish of the patient."

"Sorry, we should act now and talk about this later," the hospital doctor said. "If she dies now, it is okay. You can let her be and give her some oxygen."

I understood that it was the hospital doctor's integrity to do everything to keep her alive; however, there is the first principle of medicine, first do no harm. He does not know the whole of Ingrid and cannot perceive that this massive stroke is not something she can or even would want to survive. It is really a good time for her to go. The future holds no promise for quality of life or even a reasonable place to live. He is reacting instinctually and not able to listen to Ingrid's daughter.

The doctor is really angry with me. It is a power struggle.

"Look I know what you are thinking, and I know what you plan to do once we finish this call," I said. "But look at her chart and the advanced directive. If by any means you do not comply with the wishes of the patient and her family, you will be liable to a legal action for assault. I will back up that charge if the daughter reports this offense." This was not a bluff—there have been cases where a judge ruled against a doctor in this type of situation.

After a long, shocked pause, he said, "Okay, I give up. She is your patient, good luck." (And under his breath I heard, "F*** you.")

She did not die then, and the week that followed was quite lovely. We took her by ambulance to stay at Our Community House of Hope, the social hospice center nearby the hospital. For three or four days, friends and family came to visit her. She was in and out of consciousness, but it was a nice time. She died very gracefully and without the violence of aggressive treatment that goes far beyond keeping it simple.

Dying is an art,
like everything else.
— Sylvia Plath

20. Errol: A simple request for dignity

ERROL WAS A MAN WHO PROFOUNDLY TOUCHED MANY of us in my town. I first met him when I was doing volunteer work at the free clinic in Thousand Oaks. He was an African American man with severe cerebral palsy. It took him half an hour to get dressed in the morning. He was very bright, but his speech was off, and because of his physical disabilities one might think he was also mentally challenged, but that was hardly the case. He had worked in the tech industry in New York. Friends had asked him to come to the West Coast because the weather was better for him. When he got here, nothing panned out and he wasn't doing very well.

I accepted him as a patient probono at my office. He needed medicine for his muscle spasms and blood pressure. We got to know him well over the next 15 years. Errol never complained about his misshapen and burdensome body. He was sensitive to how others saw him, but simply accepted their reactions without judgment, which was quite a remarkable talent. I had witnessed other patients in my office waiting room quickly turn away when they saw him, and then look back with a pained expression not knowing what to do. His body was bent and difficult to move; yet if you looked beyond his appearance, you could see a gentle, affectionate, and bright being. Adversity in his case brought inner strength, with the courage to be and hope no matter what. He was quite the package of contrasts.

One day Errol fell and broke his neck. I went to see him in the intensive care unit after a surgical repair of the fracture. I asked him how he was doing. He told me, "There's a place of light inside. If I stay there, I'm okay. If I come out of there, it's impossible." He had such resilience.

Errol ended up living in his own small apartment at a place called Many Mansions, a facility for disabled and elderly people who don't have much money. He had an expressive flair for life, served as an editor for Many Mansions' newspaper, and once gave me a whole folio of romantic poetry.

One day when I saw him for a consultation in my office, I asked, "How's your love life, Errol?" He gave me a big smile and said, "There is always someone to be with from time to time." He was seriously disabled, but he still had romantic interludes. Little love affairs came his way. He was extraordinarily determined, intelligent, resourceful, open, and a gentleman—a much-loved member of his community.

Then came another bad fall and this time Errol was wedged between his bed and the wall and was unable to free himself. With no cell phone or other means for getting in touch with anyone, he lay on the floor for a full three days before someone came to see him and found him. He had a large hole where the muscles of his buttock and thigh had died, wedged hard against the wall. It took multiple surgeries and weeks of rehabilitation to repair the damage.

Weeks later, when he was out of the hospital, I was curious, so I asked him, "What did you do for those three days lying there trapped against the wall?" He explained that he had been walking through Japanese cities with artists and writers as well as traveling the countryside with haiku poets like Basho. His love of Japanese culture and people plus his highly developed imagination saved his sanity.

Spring is passing.
Birds cry, and a fish's eyes
are filled with tears.

~

Summer grasses!
All that remains
of the warriors' dreams
— Basho

Remember that Errol was physically deformed. Health professionals are no different from other people and many never get beyond the exterior to see the good, wise, sensitive, kind being within a deformed body. In a very polite and firm way, Errol always maintained his dignity. He would call me as he was recovering in hospital and say, "They're not treating me well." He'd tell me about it, and I'd go and talk to them. Without trying, Errol was always teaching lessons about dignity.

One day I got a call from the emergency room. Errol had had a stroke and collapsed in his bathwater. I went to the ER and there was a neurologist who was also the chief of staff of the hospital. Errol had no relatives and we needed to make some decisions. We stood there for a long time, reflecting on what an extraordinary man this was and how inspired some were by his attitude and his efforts.

The neurologist's every reflex was telling him to do something. The next step for Errol was intubation and intensive care. We stood there together a while longer, questioning what he would prefer. I knew he wouldn't want to be in intensive care. He was not functioning well before the stroke, and if he did survive, he would certainly come out of intensive care worse than when he went in. Intensive care units have saved many people, and I appreciate that, but at the end of life when the body is already failing, no one comes off that equipment and does well.

Before the matrix of technical options began, we were able to stop and take that moment of care. Perhaps it was because of my love for Errol. It brought clarity to our medical decision making. We didn't get into the fear mode — the do mode. We realized, just let him be, and in that, dignify his life. He expired shortly afterward. It was our gracious gesture, which suited Errol perfectly. It takes courage for a doctor to ignore the demands of technology and simply be human.

There is that voice
that doesn't use words.
Listen.
— Rumi

21. Andrea: Medical ignorance of the possibility of a peaceful departure

AT HER REQUEST, I MET PRIVATELY WITH ONE OF THE volunteers during a hospice training program. Andrea was in her thirties, and her husband of a similar age had recently died of an extremely aggressive cancer in the intensive care unit at UCLA hospital. Afterward, she went to be with her father who was also dying, but not surrounded by the cold technology of the hospital. Her father was at home with hospice care. It was like night and day for her. In the hospital ICU there is no space for conversation, for love, for time, or for grieving. In home hospice care, love can grow, making grief less a feeling of aloneness.

Andrea showed me a letter from the medical director of the UCLA hospital ICU, challenging the concept that death can be peaceful. She had written to him, wondering if there had been a time in the aggressive treatment of her husband when it was clear that the cancer was not curable, that he could have gone home to die in peace like her father.

In his response to her, the medical director initially scolded her for not appreciating the aggressive treatments to save the life of the young man. She showed me the letter that she had written, and in fact, she had expressed sincere appreciation for all the scientific treatment. She was not complaining, she was simply wondering if there had been a window for things to be different and more human in his last days.

The director's ignorance did not stop with his misreading of the intention of her letter. He went on to challenge the very experience that she'd had with her dad. He stated with his full medical authority that peaceful deaths are an illusion. He described the agony of labored, desperate breathing, the confusion, the pain, and the irritability that is, in his presumably expert opinion, always present in the last days.

In response, all I could propose to her was that perhaps this was all the UCLA medical ICU director had ever seen. His experience is typical of deaths in the intensive care unit. Maybe this is a symptom of how poorly our society tends to see death. And perhaps this is why even a timely death can be so painful and, over time, destructive to relatives and friends.

22. Vivienne: The simplicity of solitude

VIVIENNE WAS AN INTELLIGENT, ENERGETIC, MUCH loved, and respected elderly woman with a close family circle. She had single-handedly raised five very successful sons in an East Coast city. Her husband was mentally ill, so it was up to her to support, educate, and guide her sons.

The boys had all migrated to California, and as their mother got older, they bought her a lovely condo near the lake and shops in Westlake Village. She had numerous grandchildren who loved her and wanted her to be at all their school, artistic, and sporting events. There was competition between the various sons, daughters in law, and grandchildren for Grandma's presence.

Could there be too much family love for one person?

As I came to know Vivienne, I was surprised by the answer. She felt suffocated and overwhelmed by the attention and demands of being the epic loving mother and grandmother. Her friends envied her close and adoring family, no one understood her need for solitude. From time to time she had to escape to Las Vegas for a few days to enjoy being by herself.

There can be joy in solitude and pain in too much togetherness. Whole books have been written about the need to find the time to be with ourselves and no one else. During the summer after my first year in medical school, I did a psychiatric externship at the Langley Porter Neuropsychiatric in San Francisco. The chief resident, Dr. Pierre Mornell, was a good teacher. He gave us a formula for understanding human life. It has stuck with me all these years. He taught us that if you want to understand human life, look at it as S.O.S. by which he meant that our lives are defined by three distinct relationships — to Society, to Others, and to Self. The relationship to the self is where we have full control and choice. All the wise ones agree that it is in this relationship that we can discover the most profound and consistent enjoyments of life.

"Who has time for that?" is the common complaint when talking about our relationship to our self. Vivienne didn't have time for it. She had many so-called golden chains — the best social and interpersonal life, many gifts, and well-deserved successes. She was the envy of all yet had no time for cultivating self-knowledge.

During the few years that I took care of Vivienne as her primary doctor and occasional psychologist, I came to admire her inner strength and uncomplaining approach to everything. She appreciated my understanding of her need to escape to Las Vegas from time to time and her lack of constructive solitude. Taking time to wonder — to be aware and feel the goodness of existence for no reason — is food for the heart. Vivienne was a bit heart sick with the irony of too much good stuff surrounding her.

One day Vivienne came in for an urgent visit. She had gradually become weak and fatigued over a number of months. She sensed that something was very wrong. Over the next few weeks, she was diagnosed with an aggressive incurable cancer. She was dying. Her sons desperately wanted her to embrace chemotherapy to squeeze out a few more months with her. They were fearful, frantic, and frenzied in their attempts to find the best possible treatment for her anywhere in the country. These five men who were all very bright and successful were not going to stand by and let her die at home without the best treatments in the United States. Her local cancer specialists had nothing to offer so they supported the sons' research and suggestions. It is hard for any doctor to not offer anything including expensive futile experimental care. But Vivienne was not buying any of it. She wanted to be at home to depart in peace and awareness of her life's passing.

I was in the very awkward position of understanding the depth of Vivienne's fatigue and her clarity around not increasing her suffering to fight the cancer. She was not depressed. In fact, the cancer had given her the precious solitude she desired, even if it was not the best way to get time for herself.

At home, she finally enjoyed reflective time without the rounds of social obligations. Her sons saw this but did not understand it. For her to die was unacceptable to them. They were sarcastic with me about her decisions toward palliative care rather than curative care even though they understood that these decisions were made with the best advice of her oncologists. They wondered why it was not equally unacceptable to me, her primary doctor. They feared that everything that could be done was not being done.

"Do no harm" is the first principle of medicine, but in the heat of battle, it is easy to ignore this old fashioned wisdom. If medical decisions come from fear, legal concerns, or money issues, mistakes are inevitable. Wisdom in medical decisions has to come from a place of clarity and kindness within for all the players. My clear support for Vivienne's most fundamental need for dignity and peace was an expression of this principle. To pursue more treatments would be harmful to her spirit, and not supportive of her needs.

After a rather peaceful home-hospice experience, Vivienne died. I was invited to the religious service and burial. Her sons were still slightly suspicious of me and disappointed in me.

Many of my patients have experienced the presence of departed relatives and friends. These experiences seem to be helpful to them. I appreciated the effect they have on the person. Up to this point in my life, I had not had that type of experience, but I never questioned or judged the occurrence for others. So it was much to my surprise and delight—when I left the burial service—that I felt and almost saw Vivienne in the sky with diamonds, so to speak. She was free and quite at peace and seemed to be expressing gratitude to me for my understanding of her golden chains. Free, free at last she seemed to be saying. It was a brief and very pleasant experience and the only one that I've ever had. Perhaps it was my own appreciation for having been true to Vivienne's understanding of herself.

23. Our Community House of Hope

IF DYING CAN HAPPEN AT HOME, FANTASTIC—THAT'S often the best—but sometimes it can't happen that way. Some communities and cultures have an incredible fabric of support among family, friends, and strangers, which alleviates the burden of care. This is not prevalent in the United States, where a typical family may be scattered across the country.

To alleviate this need for care, I helped found an end-of-life social hospice home that supported evolving end-of-life needs where I live in Southern California. For five years, Our Community House of Hope (OCHH) provided a good place for people at the end of life, before closing its doors due to a lack of sustainable funding. OCHH was not labelled as a place to go and die, but an end-of-living place. It provided a tremendous benefit to our community.

The house was set up like a regular home, with comfortable bedrooms, a living room, a proper kitchen, and a tranquil backyard. During its five years of operation, more than 200 people spent their last days there because they had no other place to be at the end of their life, due to lack of resources or because it was not working out where they were living, or they could not find suitable caregivers.

The costs at OCHH were low and operations were supported by many volunteers and local charities. Families could be there with their loved one, and they were welcome to treat the house as their own. They could cook if they wanted to and spend time together as if they were at home. In that space, each family had the time, space, and privacy to be together and focus on love in a way that fosters a good departure.

Currently, there are several cities across the country that are looking to set up social-care hospices modeled on Our Community House of Hope. Some of the proceeds from this book will go to support the evolution of more such houses.

What if the world were filled with small or large, private or public houses of hope where the force of love and kindness could give all of us the space for this rite of passage — to die in peace? It would be a lot less costly than a hospital's rite of passage to death, which has become the default. The kindness and love of a house of hope would nourish all involved, and if everyone knew it was an option, it would remove the fear of being isolated and dying alone. It would offer one less reason to fear death.

Some of the people who came to OCHH to die did not die. In the company of acceptance, kindness, home-cooked food, a lovely garden, and other brave souls, they just got better. It was wonderful to see them leave the house having not yet reached their real shelf life.

Having the option to be in such a home as OCHH can present a wonderful alternative to the misdirected and expensive medical ritual of keeping patients alive in the ICU of a hospital when indeed they just need a place to rest in peace before dying. I cited earlier the book called *Birth Without Violence* by Dr. Leboyer, published in 1974, whose simple notion was that the bright lights and rough handling of newborns was too violent. Soft lighting, not swaddling the body in rough cloth, bringing to the mother's chest quickly and then to a warm bath produced remarkable results. Babies were much more settled and smiled more frequently, they seemed happier and so did the mothers. There was a wave of home births and the development of birthing centers after that milestone book. Why not the same consciousness and care at the other end of life?

Simplicity is the ultimate sophistication.
— Leonardo da Vinci

UNDERSTANDING 4

Resolve Regrets

IN ORDER TO LEAVE WITHOUT REGRET, IT IS IMPORTANT to understand that medicine is not just about caring for our biology. As I have matured as a doctor, a model of medicine that I learned about in medical school has provided a much-needed wider lens to get to know a patient and prevent regretful angry departures. This lens is the bio-psycho-social model coined by the eminent internist and psychiatrist George Engel. His model simply states that every condition of health or illness has three dimensions:

- *Biological*—what is happening in the body;
- *Psychological*—what is happening in the thoughts, emotions, intentions, and imagination of the person;
- *Social*—the cultural context of the person.

These three dimensions interact with one another. To fully understand a person, we need to pay attention to each one. Of course, this requires real conversations over time. Time is money in medicine these days, so it requires a little courage for a doctor to buck the system and take time to really get to know someone. Not only does this provide good medical intelligence, but it is an opportunity for both people to feel some kindness and gain empathy — necessary human resources either in the healing process or in the departure process.

We can find a path to letting go of the things we regret or didn't get to do. One may feel some regret that the place of peace was neglected, given that life is busy. But fortunately, peace can soon replace a regret or anger.

In resolving regrets, we can appreciate all that we did and let go of all we did not do or all we did not become. When it comes to lingering animosities and hatreds, expressing gratitude can be easier than we might think, especially when there is not so much time left to dwell on personal problems with others. The goodness of existence becomes more palpable as we get ready for departure.

Anger is a natural step in coming to face death.
— Elizabeth Kübler-Ross

Just don't get stuck there.
— John Horton

24. Mr. Daniels: Never enough

NOT SO LONG AGO, A VERY WEALTHY PATIENT, MR. Daniels came to say goodbye to me because he heard we were shutting down our practice. We had been through a number of his medical adventures caused by his pushing through exhaustion with the use of caffeine and alcohol. His ability to put in long days and nights to do more work than anyone was the source of his financial success. His strong body was equal to his strong mind and determination.

Once I got a call from a doctor in Hong Kong to tell me Mr. Daniels was in liver failure and asking if there was any history of liver infections or tumors. He was calling because my patient insisted he call me before doing any invasive diagnostic procedures. I asked the Hong Kong doctor if he knew how much coffee and alcohol Mr. Daniels had been consuming in recent weeks and months. Understandably, in the emergency situation, he had not asked about this seemingly mundane medical history. Half a day later, he called back to agree with the patient's request for rest, reasonable nutrition, and no more caffeine and alcohol for a while. His liver was able to regenerate quickly as it had in past episodes.

Weeks later, Mr. Daniels came to say goodbye bearing a gift of understanding to give to me. He had been thinking of a handful of super wealthy people he knew. Each of them became wealthy for very different reasons. Some were brilliant, creative innovators, some had family fortunes, some made a lucky investment, and some like Mr. Daniels could work harder and longer than others. What he wanted to share with me is that they all had one thing in common. Not one of them felt they had enough, so each day was a stressful struggle for more. Fortunately Mr. Daniels was not a victim of this affliction. He was able to enjoy the time for rest, relaxation, recreation, and reflection that I had been prescribing over our time together.

25. Mr. James: Do you qualify for an early departure?

"DO YOU QUALIFY FOR AN EARLY DEPARTURE?" I found myself asking this of a hospice patient recently. If life is winding down, is there a way to somehow qualify to depart without enduring the crush of a tragic, slow, or painful ending?

Mr. James had always been warm and kind toward me during his many years as a patient in our medical practice. He was almost apologetic about the degree of difficulty he had experienced due to chronic back pain and sciatica. His courage and hopefulness were inspiring — despite unsuccessful surgeries, he stayed focused on what he could do physically to keep moving. He had been an active man but gradually took to his bed because sitting, standing, and walking caused debilitating pain.

By the time Mr. James entered the hospice stage of care, he was completely bed-bound. Even moving him out of bed to sit in his garden brought on hours of excruciating pain. He had given up on the strongest pain medications because they made him feel dopey and depressed. He could best manage his pain in bed with non-narcotic medications and rest.

Lovely photos that he had taken on adventurous holidays with his family lined the walls of his home. Despite having good help in his home and remaining amicable with his wife, being bed-bound hurt his dignity. If only he could walk, go for a drive, or visit his children he might have managed to have a few more enjoyable years.

One day the hospice nurse called and requested that I visit and suggested that I prescribe medication for depression. The hospice nurses always encouraged Mr. James to eat more and be more active, perhaps not appreciating how painful it was for him to be carried to the garden or put in a car. His pain kept him in the jail of his one room. I talked with his wife privately and found that she did not find him depressed, just very frustrated with his immobility and chronic pain. She was certainly in sync with his desire for his jail term of suffering to end sooner rather than later. He wasn't suicidal, just exhausted.

I probed for depression and found none. He had his usual affable, clear, and grounded sense of himself as well as gratitude for a life well lived. He expressed a sweet love for his wife and current caretakers as well as for his son, daughter, and grandchildren. However, he was painfully regretful that he had not had a better relationship with his son as a child. His son had developmental difficulties, and he had found it challenging to support him without judgement. He felt he could have been a better parent and didn't relate to his son much as an adult.

I encouraged him to reach out and have a daily conversation with his son. What did he have to lose at this point? He stepped up and made the calls. Their relationship transformed over the next week, and I was delighted to discover he had resolved his regrets in his role as a parent.

During our next visit it was more obvious to me that his profound fatigue was solely from carrying the burden of long days and nights with limited mobility and no hope for change. He no longer carried any burden of regret, just the burdensome body he carried.

In the affection and mutual respect of our long relationship, I asked him a strange question: "Do you qualify for an early departure?"

I was as surprised as he was when I asked it. It felt like a question from an airline employee standing before the boarding gate of a soon to be departing plane wondering who would be welcomed onto it first. The question sounds a little absurd, it certainly led to a humorous exchange.

I entered into this unique, never previously performed assessment by reviewing the understanding Mr. James and I had discussed in detail only a few weeks before. He was sure of accepting death as a natural thing, without fear or hesitation, he was always doing it his way and he did well at keeping it simple. Now, there was only one last question left for him to understand: what might you feel about leaving as you depart? I shared with him a poem by the Indian poet Kabir (1440–1518):

When you were born, you cried, and the people rejoiced.
Live in such a manner that when you die,
the people cries and you rejoice.

The next 10 minutes were a delight for both of us. The laughing joy of Kabir's expression was abundant. We were transformed by the depth of his peace. It was an unexpected and wonderful occasion, like a gentle cooling rain on a very hot afternoon in summer. We could feel the promise of relief and comfort now present in the air.

After our exchange, I declared that he did indeed meet the criteria for an early departure and left with two promises: that I would return within a week or two, and that he could, with my support, eat less to hasten his departure.

When the hospice informed me two days later that Mr. James had died, I was stunned and silent and felt both the tears of sadness and the laughter of joy Kabir had described so long ago. It took a week for me to connect with his hospice nurse who expressed surprise that he died so suddenly. I told her of our last meeting. Her response was sweet, “So, he was on the runway for that early departure, who knew!”

What is this process of letting go as death approaches? American medicine and American society in general are rather notorious for not embracing end-of-life options. We fight, deny, ignore, and finally are resigned to death, without entertaining the simple human possibilities. So many experiences point to the importance of conscious choices even in the very last days of life.

26. Ralph: A departure in anger

IN JAPAN, COMMON WISDOM SAYS THAT IT IS DANGERous to have always been healthy because when old age and illness come, it will be difficult not to be disappointed and bitter. Ralph proved that to be true.

When I first met Ralph, I was impressed with his vitality and athletic fitness. He had the deeply sun-tanned good looks of the seasoned Floridian tennis pro he had been for over 30 years. He came to see me while visiting his son in Washington, DC, near Bethesda. He had developed some painful symptoms of urinary obstruction.

Ralph was quite upset with his symptoms, which he claimed had begun during his visit. He was edgy and belligerent toward his son who attended the consultation. It was as if he was protesting his son's family life in Washington as a government employee. Why was he not living in Florida near him, teaching tennis, swimming, drinking fresh orange juice, and simply enjoying the good life?

His moderate symptoms of prostate swelling did not improve with standard medicine, so he went to see a well-known Washington urologist who determined he needed a small surgery. This angered Ralph, but as his symptoms worsened, he really had no choice. The surgery was done successfully at Suburban Hospital where I could also attend him. His son and daughter-in-law were there to support him, but his attitude remained terrible. No matter what we did to make Ralph understand the ordinariness of his medical problem, calmness and balance seemed to elude him. Anger, blame, and misery are not good ingredients for healing, so his seemingly simple infection lingered, then got worse.

Ralph was a man who was never ill, and from his point of view nothing was being done right. He lived a good life in Florida — why should he suddenly get ill? His irritation seemed to suggest that he thought being in Washington caused the problem. After the successful procedure, he developed a urinary tract infection, so he had to stay in the hospital an extra few days for IV antibiotics. Generally this kind of infection is not a big deal, but it provoked an extreme searing anger in him that I, as a young doctor, had never seen before. Usually, at some point, patients become a little humble and grateful for good care, even if they are not entirely trusting what is being done for them. Having practiced medicine in rural India and lived in African villages, I was aware of how lucky he was for the ease of access to medical resources. We had a wonderful support team but none of us knew how to soothe him.

In this extreme state of being, his immune system was compromised and we watched helplessly as the infection raged on. Then suddenly he was in renal failure and just as suddenly he was dead. We were numb, sad, and felt very bad.

We had considered getting a psychiatry consult but we were convinced that he would see this as adding insult to injury. So, you people screw up and now you want to say that I am crazy, was what we imagined as his response.

His anger was, perhaps, some kind of personality disorder. He couldn't discuss his emotions or thoughts. Perhaps his anger came from fear or regret. Having never been ill, he had no capacity to deal with his own sense of helplessness and hopelessness. These twin imposters can drive our stress responses into a spasm of fight, or flight, or freeze. It was easy to blame him, but not really fair; maybe he just needed support that we had failed to give him — a failure of poor doctoring.

This was a hard lesson for me. In retrospect, I know I could have and should have taken more time to build a relationship with this man who became overwhelmed with uncertainty and fear. Now I understand that this anger might have been mitigated with more understanding.

Let's reflect on a simple very profound formula:

Uncertainty causes fear.
Unresolved fear causes anger.
Anger causes harm.

Whether it's harm to oneself or others doesn't matter: harm evokes more uncertainty, then fear, then anger, and then more harm. The only way to stop this cycle is to consciously reject the fear and lean in to find some certainty.

27. Mr. Quinn: Never too late

MR. QUINN DIED AFTER A LONG STRUGGLE TO RESOLVE his passion to change the world. In his early sixties, Mr. Quinn was a fit, athletic, idealistic man who ate well and was proud of his reliable good health. When I first met him, I was struck by how ill he seemed. He was tall and fair-skinned with kind brown eyes, and he had the dignity of a professor. The love between him and his wife was strong, he evoked both respect and compassion. Mr. Quinn worked as a chemical engineer, but his passion was social activism. He supported progressive social movements in our Washington, DC, community and even led a strike of the workers at the Suburban Hospital in Bethesda, where he and I lived.

Having always been healthy, he was bewildered, frustrated, and angry with his unexplained weakness, exhaustion, and poor mood. I quickly hospitalized him for a diagnostic work up. After a few days we still did not have a diagnosis, and he was not getting better. We transferred him to the Georgetown Diagnostic Clinic, which has an international reputation. Various specialists consulted and found a very rare kidney cancer, extremely virulent and aggressive. They couldn't do anything to treat it, so he went home to live out what was left of his life.

From our first meeting, Mr. Quinn was psychologically very challenging for me as well as for his loving wife. Throughout his life as a successful engineer and social activist, he had always been an effective leader. He was intelligent, articulate, and sincere in his political activities, but his mood had become one of searing despair. Filled with resentment, he felt abandoned and rejected by his closest friends and even his wife for reasons that had nothing to do with his cancer diagnosis.

This was in the early 1970s, and there had been a major shift in thinking among social activists. People who had been political revolutionaries were now starting to talk about cultivating consciousness as a pathway to a more profound social change than simply trying to change things externally. Basically, this philosophical shift involved encouraging people to choose kindness, empathy and justice over greed, fear, and the lust for power. I had been a social activist in medical school (even participating in a strike of medical residents for better medical care for patients) and I could now understand this issue of consciousness. It was the old question of revolution and protest versus evolution of a different sort of inclusive human consciousness.

One important thinker of that era was Marshall McLuhan, who was actually a friend of Mr. Quinn's. For Mr. Quinn, this new movement was a sign of cowardice and an intellectual cop out. He was content to argue this difference for hours, so his wife reported. His friends had begun to embrace the New Age consciousness. The alienation between Mr. Quinn and his friends became hostile, and he ultimately experienced the pain of rejection. Even after the thousands of years of our evolution from belonging to hunter-gatherer groups, rejection can feel like imminent death.

As his doctor, if I tried to talk to Mr. Quinn about this cultural change in attitude, he would become mean and condescending. His resentment and rejection seemed the most powerful forces in his life. His wife felt helpless, and she wondered how much of his bitterness had to do with the cancer. She felt it was the main cause. Certainly, it was part of the picture. I felt sorry that he might die in such a sour, bitter state when we did not have anything further to offer him.

One day, not long after he had been sent home from the Georgetown hospital, his wife called and asked me to come and see him. She wouldn't tell me on the phone why she wanted me to visit. I feared that his anger and hostility were out of control.

Wishing I was carrying a shield to protect myself, I went to see him. His wife led me through a calm, beautiful home to his bright, comfortable bedroom. When I entered, he was sleeping. She gently woke him up. His eyes were bright and shining as he came out of this seemingly peaceful rest. He began talking about a beautiful light. Then he focused on me and said, "Human being," as if he was recognizing another human being with fresh eyes. He was excited and kind in seeing me, a human being, coming from wherever he had been inside. His wife and I were both delighted by this transformation.

Then suddenly the hostility was back.

"Yes doctor what do you want?"

I did not respond to this usual attitude. He quickly went back to his calm, peaceful state. His wife looked at me and asked is this okay, meaning that he was not angry and cynical. She was not sure about his new mood and peaceful state. Was this a temporary hallucination that would fade as death continued to approach the man she dearly loved? It seemed to me that he was discovering the simplicity of his good heart. As he lost the physical, mental, and emotional energies to protest and try to change the injustices of the world, he could relax into himself.

I didn't visit again, but I talked to his wife on the phone. She told me he was in this beautiful place. Here was a man who really wanted the best for society, but he got stuck in this almost violent commitment to social change. Then at the end there was a transformation, and he came to a beautiful place of resolution. His anger had evaporated like the morning mist in the heat of the sun.

From Mr. Quinn I learned that it is literally never too late to come home to a peaceful existence.

28. Mavis: A daughter's love

WHEN I MET MAVIS, SHE WANTED A CIGARETTE. HER daughter, who had arrived that day, refused to let her smoke and phoned the hospice staff to request a visit from the doctor. It was early evening when I got the call. My initial thoughts were: "What! You have to be joking. This woman has days or hours left to live and her daughter doesn't want her to smoke? Hadn't her daughter seen any war movies? The dying soldier always gets to smoke a cigarette."

Hospice nurses know more or less how much time a person has left. This woman had hours and minutes left. I did have a fleeting thought that this might be a waste of my time on a Friday evening. I knocked on the door of a house that seemed uninhabited, with flaking paint and more weeds visible than sidewalk. A woman dressed in neat slacks and a tidy blouse greeted me with a ready smile on her face. This was the daughter who had just arrived from Boston that afternoon. I introduced myself, and she welcomed me to come in and see her mother, Mavis. I decided to take some time to assess the situation before bringing up the smoking issue.

Entering Mavis' room, I encountered another place that Dante didn't describe. Misery and filth were the companions of a woman who could barely sit up. Her presence was very fuzzy, and her brow deeply furrowed. She was altogether fragile, and her facial expressions were ugly, full of disgust and apathy. I had never seen anyone quite like her. Emaciated and unkempt, she resembled a starving stray cat more than a person. There were newspapers and books everywhere, as well as plates and dishes of days-old, partially eaten food. The daughter had just arrived late that afternoon and it was now evening.

Before asking the daughter about her issues with her mother smoking, I decided to reach out to Mavis. I carefully approached her from the left side, thinking that I would take her pulse as an excuse to make some comfortable physical contact. I noticed she wore a big ring on the middle finger of her left hand. It was really big — far too big for such a small woman. She started lifting her hand with the ring, as if she was getting ready to hit me with it. I had begun to approach very gently, but I stopped when she raised her hand.

As I retreated, I glanced at the daughter who was standing close by. She had a twinkle in her eye, confirming that yes, given the opportunity, her mother would strike this stranger with all the force of her being.

Was this old-age dementia with paranoia or her personality? The daughter explained that when she was a child, her mother would tempt the small neighborhood children with sweets. They would come close to her, sit on her lap, and then she'd smack them with the ring.

She'd been a mean woman. Her daughter knew she would die alone, and her daughter didn't think that was right. So, she came to be with her mother despite her history.

I was impressed. This woman must have done a lot of work on herself to have grown up with such a mean mother and still be willing to come and be with her at the end.

What about the cigarettes, I asked? She was worried Mavis would drop a lit cigarette into the trash, and being jet lagged, the daughter might nod off and not notice. It was a reasonable concern. Then the question became why even light up the cigarette in the first place. The daughter anticipated my question and told me that her mother would scream until the lit cigarette was in her mouth. I commented that her screaming would not only be intolerable to the daughter but also to the cockroaches who were inhabiting the room — a grim scene, indeed.

I don't remember how we resolved the cigarette thing. But it was wonderful to see this woman come to be with her mother who was not going to have a graceful departure. How touching and kind of the daughter to come. Her mother did die that night, peacefully.

This example makes me reflect on forgiveness.

I do small groups for my patients to discover the natural healing process for emotional and mental trauma. We have come up with an understanding of forgiveness, which is part of the need to resolve regrets at the end of life.

Forgiveness is not rationalizing or dismissing the harm done. It is not letting the person or persons off for the pain or fear or frustrations caused by their actions. It is reaching a place within oneself where what happened no longer causes any inner or outer suffering. This is real forgiveness. It takes effort and time to reach this destination, and it is a gift mostly to oneself.

Let us forgive each other.
Only then will we live in peace.
— Leo Tolstoy

29. Compassion

THERE IS SYMPATHY, WHICH IS NICE BUT SOMEWHAT superficial. "My condolences . . . do you like my new shoes?" Then there is empathy — when you really understand another person's thoughts, feelings, and intentions. They feel you can appreciate them and understand them — it is a deeper connection.

Then there is compassion. Even though this person is suffering a great deal, you can see deep within them a possibility — a life force that has those qualities that are home for us — when you can see that in the depths of a person suffering — it is a beautiful connection to our common humanity.

If you are with a person who is suffering or approaching departure, you can allow yourself to really understand what they are thinking, feeling, and intending, even though it might be quite dark and unpleasant. This is compassion as described by Roshi Joan Halifax. People often fight the person suffering, insisting that they need to have a positive attitude, insisting they be grateful, insisting they eat or do other things they don't want to do. That doesn't help the person to feel understood.

In allowing yourself to understand the person, however, you don't entirely leave yourself behind because afterward, you need to be able to return to the baseline qualities of yourself. Otherwise, you can wind up overwhelmed, running away, or fighting. As Halifax puts it: living in the shadow of death brings out your passion to live each day fully. It sounds almost trite to say that, but it is so seldom practiced in our culture. Often when people go to visit a sick person, they want to fill the air with conversation, which, while they mean well, doesn't afford the person compassion.

Compassion benefits everyone and can be learned. It's a skill that comes from cultivating wisdom. Some of us don't know how to balance our checkbook or do our taxes, but we can learn if we have the motivation. Same goes for compassion.

30. Deborah: Does complaining ever end?

I HAVE A PATIENT FRIEND WHO IS A BRILLIANT PUBLIC relations expert. She had asked me if I would care for her mother, Deborah. She warned me that it wasn't going to be easy, as her mother had experienced a lot of suffering. Deborah had lived through many tragedies, but she was a resilient Jewish woman. Over a few years as her primary doctor, I came to appreciate and respect her. She suffered from various ills and personal losses but maintained a strong spirit. She also loved to complain. After a few years of tolerating her everyday misery, bad news came in the form of a brain tumor. It felt like we were going to be in for a very rough ride. The tumor was aggressive, inoperable, and the radiation treatment made her feel wretched. She eventually decided on home hospice.

When Deborah returned home, we all expected the worst—more suffering and pain. But once she was at home with good hospice care, she started to flourish. Friends came to see her, and she experienced an extraordinary renaissance of wonder, realizing that many people loved her. She began to learn, to enjoy, and even feel grateful. She was delighted by her rebirth and so was her daughter. Her turnaround in replacing regrets with wonder was really quite something to see—just as each day is complete for a child, with all the regrets of the day before gone.

Then one day her daughter called and told me she was reluctant to visit Deborah at home because she'd complain about everything her caregivers did. We had very competent and kind people taking care of her, but in her mind, nothing they did was right. The caregivers were so fed up that they wanted to leave.

The daughter didn't know whether to cry or scream. Deborah accused her of not being compassionate, attentive, and available to her, which was far from the truth. The daughter had been running her own substantial business from her mother's bedside, doing all of the grocery shopping and errands, picking up and administering medicine, reading books aloud to Deborah, tending to all her needs and whims. One day, Deborah had asked for some rye bread. Her daughter honored her request and visited three different bakeries to find the right bread, only to be met with Deborah's unappreciative response: "I wanted rye bread with seeds."

That was the last straw. Under this continual flow of complaints, she'd had enough and walked out, unwilling to take further assault. In Yiddish, complaining is called "kvetching" and it was a habit Deborah had had all her life. She was an expert at it to the point where it dominated her personality.

We had a crisis. Without her daughter and the caregivers, she would need to go to a nursing home. That kind of move in her fragile condition would be an ordeal for everyone. I proposed a family counseling session.

Deborah's daughter, son, and daughter-in-law, and I assembled around Deborah's bed with the intention of gently confronting her chronic kvetching. She immediately picked up on their frustration and accused me of setting her up to be attacked by her family. I managed to persuade her that was not something I would allow, that we were only looking for clarity and understanding so that her life could continue to evolve to embrace the new-found inner freedom she was enjoying. I told her there was an obstacle between her and those trying to help her that I was convinced she did not see. I framed it as another opportunity to discover more goodness in herself.

Ultimately, we had a delightful hour of understanding that the wisdom of the heart is more powerful than a lifetime habit of complaining. We discussed how if a complaint is reasonable, then it's no more than a request. If you are standing on my foot and I ask you to move, it is a reasonable request that is easily actionable. We helped Deborah see that her complaining was a habit born of all the suffering and pain she had experienced. It was an attitude based on the absence of heartfelt contentment and kindness.

Surrounded by the obvious love of her so called "accusers" at her bedside, Deborah managed to understand the distinction between a reasonable request and the soul-numbing approach of complaining about everything. It was remarkable indeed, almost miraculous, that after that one session Deborah was able to dwell in the appreciation of her heart rather than the superhighway of kvetching.

One day you will look back and see that all along you were blooming.

— Morgan Harper Nichols

31. Rachel: Trans-generational trauma

SOMETIMES THERE ARE EVENTS IN OUR LIVES OR even in the lives of our ancestors that interfere with a regret-free death.

Back in Bethesda I was asked to care for Rachel, an elderly Jewish widow who had been admitted to an upscale nursing home for dementia and behavioral problems. A retired accountant, Rachel had been doing well through most of her seventies, staying socially active and mentally sharp. She had a network of friends, doted on her grandchildren, and did the bookkeeping for her son and daughter-in-law with whom she'd lived since the death of her husband. She had been proud of aging well, and everything was fine until Rachel's cognition started to decline as part of advancing Alzheimer's disease. She could no longer understand numbers and her short-term memory started to fail. It was a shattering loss for a woman whose sense of identity had been shaped in large part by her mental prowess.

Rachel's mental diminishment triggered a storm of fear, frustration, and anger in this once kindly and convivial woman. She blamed her family for her decline with a fury that descended into paranoia, as she became convinced that they were trying to kill her. She even took to trawling the neighborhood to try and enlist people in stopping her family from "robbing" and "poisoning" her. Medications prescribed by Rachel's doctors failed to regulate her emotions and, after a time, she refused them altogether. Rachel's son was a judge and his wife a psychiatrist. They both had demanding careers and were raising a family of their own. They were unable to continue caring for Rachel under such difficult conditions, so they decided it was time for her to move into a nursing home.

This was where I met Rachel for the first time. A handsome older woman who must once have been a young beauty, she wore a stylish dress and was meticulously groomed. Yet there was nothing attractive about her demeanor, all anger, resentment, and brittleness and that was how she remained throughout her time in the nursing home.

Rachel's social and emotional isolation at the nursing home was absolute. None of the group activities — no matter how highly cultured — could tempt her, and none of the residents sparked her interest. Nothing her kind caregivers said or did soothed her. Even the tranquilizers that were snuck into her food to ease her inner turmoil had no effect.

I was still a young pup in my medical practice — enthusiastic and energetic, but with little hands-on medical experience — and no experience at all with age-related dementia. Had

I known more about the psychosocial dimensions of suffering, I would have made the connection between Rachel's seemingly unreasoning anger and the unexpressed terror she must have been experiencing in her new and diminished state. No longer able to rely on her brain to make sense of her world, she must have felt as if her entire life was crumbling into chaos and uncertainty. Terrifying indeed.

I also might have suspected what I now feel was almost certainly true: this formerly amiable Jewish widow was in the grip of deep, transgenerational Holocaust trauma, surfacing now, when her psychological defenses were weak. Armed with these insights, we might have found some way to support Rachel emotionally and help her reach a place of more acceptance and peace. We might even have arranged for hospice care at home before she became so consumed by fury and dementia that she needed to be institutionalized. As it was, I could only stand by helplessly watching this fearful and traumatized woman terrorize nursing staff and family alike.

Rachel had only been in the nursing home for a few months when she developed a serious liver infection, went into a semi-coma, and was hospitalized. It was a small mercy for her and her family. With no treatment for her viral hepatitis, the specialists gave her a few days to live at most. Her family and I decided that the kindest thing would be to forego heroic interventions and allow her to dehydrate quickly and die peacefully. This decision was not relayed to the hospital intern on duty the night of her hospital admission. He put in an IV and pumped her full of fluids and vitamins to revive her.

The next morning, to our astonishment and dismay, Rachel was awake, energized — and boiling mad. When I entered her hospital room, she was berating the well-meaning young nurse who was standing by her bedside.

"What's happening?" I asked.

"Take that one by the throat and slam her against the wall," Rachel snarled.

Her son, his wife, and I were shocked and shaken. Since Rachel seemed to know who I was, I decided to give it my last, best shot. Leaning toward her, I told Rachel that — short of killing her nurse — I wanted to do whatever I could to make her comfortable. Rachel paused and regarded me intently. Encouraged, I eagerly doubled down. With as much care and conviction as I could, I offered her these words: "Whatever I can do to help, please let me know."

Expressionless, she barked, "Have you ever thought about suicide? Maybe you should try it."

That was it. There was nothing more any of us could do for this furious, dying woman. It was very sad to leave her room together, the three us, and know that the peace of death would probably come with little appreciation from Rachel.

Rachel's revival was short-lived. The fluids pumped into her had caused her heart and kidneys to fail while her liver infection raged on. Soon she slipped back into a coma, dying quietly later that day. Her passing was both sad and a relief. During her last months, Rachel was so punishing to be around that her family had been guiltily looking forward to her departure. Had Rachel been able to resolve whatever fears she was carrying, her time in the departure lounge might have been less dreadful — or even pleasant.

A doctor gets used to feeling helpless on occasion, but it's rare that I've felt unable to have any positive impact at all. As it was, Rachel's story became a priceless lesson for me in the importance of paying heed to the psychological dimensions of suffering early on, and not to discount experiences in the distant past, including trauma in past generations.

I now know that even when a disease is irreversible, there is always the possibility for emotional healing: using psychotherapy, dream work, rituals, and other holistic approaches that open a door to our psyche. We neglect the psychological and social dimensions of health at our peril. Traumas and fears that are not dealt with are like sharks in the deep — shadowy creatures that can darken and breach our psyches when we least expect them — a stealth attack.

Looking back, I wonder how much of her agony was fear? Trans-generational holocaust PTSD? Young children have no hesitation in telling someone that they are afraid. But as we age, we are taught that being afraid is unacceptable. Some fears are so big that there are no words to convey them. There is still time. Toward the end, it is okay to feel afraid, just as you did as a small child. We need to understand that even in the face of cognitive decline and dementia, suffering is not inevitable (see the story of Robert Young, page 172.)

32. The grieving process

WE MAY GRIEVE AT TWO TIMES: WHEN WE OR OUR loved one worsen over a period of weeks or days before death and then, those who remain grieve following a death. Let me address both of those periods.

During the period before death

One of the obstacles to coming to a place of peace is our discomfort with the prospect of feeling grief. Anticipating the grief of dying or losing loved ones can certainly color the last days. If we can understand more about the capacity that we have to successfully navigate the waves of grief, experiencing death can be easier — both for the dying and for those who are present. We can see grief as an element on the same scale as love, where they are both part of our emotional experience, and definitely something we all have capacity for.

There is a tool from The Inner Game that is helpful in stepping back from overwhelming situations. These are called The

Control Questions. The first question is, in this situation, what are the things you do not control and cannot control? This is always a long and humbling list as you attempt to take part in the control of the hospital care or as a caregiver at home.

The second question is: What are you now controlling? This is a much shorter list. Getting caught up in trying to control things that we cannot control is frustrating. This can cause stress reactions that tax the very limited menu of the stress system—fight, flee, freeze, or flock. The tendency to flock, especially in the crisis of someone dying, can mean consulting with a group of people and abdicating your own decision making. It's important not to sacrifice your role in caring for your loved one in going along with the others.

The third question to ask yourself—after you've exhausted the answers to the first two—allows for a reflective, still space: what can you control in this situation that you are not already controlling? This is perhaps the most pertinent question to come to peace with your need to feel in control. In many instances, you will find that your ability to control how you or your loved one departs is out of your hands.

As a bystander, don't be afraid of looking forward without regret while at the same time being fully present with the person while they are dying. It is not bad to have two things going on. You don't have to make flight plans. You are investing in your future. It is not a betrayal of love or loyalty to consider future plans when a loved one is dying. It can be comforting for the dying person to consider what that space can become and encourage their loved ones and caretakers to think about what they will do afterward.

Our greatest freedom is our ability
to choose our attitude.
— Viktor Frankl

Grief after death

Grieving after the death of a loved one is typically a solitary activity in Western cultures. It is something we do behind closed doors, sometimes with the help of a therapist. This is not typical in more traditional cultures, where people are often given a prolonged period filled with rituals and observances that help them stay connected to their sorrow, process it, and let go.

Sadness is as natural as happiness, yet in America it's not considered respectable. Instead, we have something called toxic positivity. The torture of having to always be positive is an unnecessary burden in the dance of grief — and life for that matter. It is human to feel sad, to feel glad, to feel pain, to feel pleasure, to feel alone, to feel cared for, and to feel a loss that may seem unending.

Francis Weller's book, *The Wild Edge of Sorrow: Rituals of Renewal and the Sacred Work of Grief,* sheds light on grief as a very acceptable and important component of our humanity. He provides overwhelming evidence that grieving is best done with the help of one's community.

The support we need might not be therapy behind closed doors — it can be as simple as having a good conversation with a friend of sound mind. In Weller's words, "To be human is to know loss in its many forms. Even though sorrow never disappears, it can make a deeper connection to the currents of life . . . it connects somehow to sources of wonder and solace."

Sufficient time is required to fully express our grief. We cannot simply take a few days of bereavement leave and expect to be done. It's not in our nature. Just as love accompanies us and seeks our acceptance, so too does grief. If we avoid grief, we can become numb to the joys and sorrows of the world. When we grieve, we almost need a menu of options, things we can do to help ourselves divert our habits of wanting to relate to that person or thing we loved, to give our focus to something else. Weller highlights this with a beautiful metaphor:

Grief and love are sisters, woven together from the beginning.
There is no love that does not contain loss
and no loss that is not a reminder of what we once held close.
— Francis Weller

Initially, grief comes like waves in the ocean, and when a wave sweeps over you, it's best to just let it take you down without fighting it. Fight is futile because the wave is stronger than you are, but once it breaks, you can easily resurface for air and stability.

Similarly, when waves of sadness sweep over you, it's best to just allow yourself to be sad. There's no need to struggle because that wave of sadness will break and you'll feel better. Over time, the waves become less frequent and intense. Over time, the waves cease, and you can dwell in fond memories and gratitude. There is nothing trite about saying that it's better to have loved and lost than never to have loved at all. To know love is to be fully human.

Love for the person you lost can dance in your heart, but you need to place other people and activities in the emotional, mental, and physical space that the loved one occupied in your life. You can look around and perhaps see the qualities you admired in that person in other people. Your sphere of love and understanding can expand. If that space remains empty for too long, there is the danger that confusion, doubt, fear, anger, and hopelessness can fill that vacuum. Nature does not like a vacuum.

Grief can be the garden of compassion.
If you keep your heart open through everything,
your pain can become your greatest ally
in your life's search for love and wisdom.
— Rumi

UNDERSTANDING 5

Discover Peace

THERE ARE TWO PIECES TO FINDING PEACE IN DEPARTing. One is resolving regrets and coming to peace with what your life has been. The other piece is discovering the peace inherent to the human heart.

When all is said and done, the end resembles the beginning of life. Remember that effort to take the first breath I described in my most profound lecture in medical school? That strength came from the life force as a gift. As an infant being born, we just accept that as it comes to us. Then we rest peacefully, comfortably, and safely. At the end, the peace of the life force will find us when we have nothing else to do.

Certainly, the more we have cultivated inner peace in all of our prior days, the easier it will be to dwell in peace in our last days. The body shuts down gradually if death is not sudden. Many patients and families are afraid that death will come from suffocation because the lungs cease to function. Some people do well with oxygen if they have lung disease, but most of us do not need extra oxygen. Always, the heart ceases function before the lungs, so the brain will not know about the breath ending. As you have seen from the patient stories, the last breath can be as smooth as silk.

I do not think that this peace is deserved or a reward for good behavior. It is not a belief because the kindness and love of this peace is beyond belief. It seems too good to be true. It is in this peace that we find freedom from suffering. This is why death is celebrated in many cultures.

The twin imposters of hopelessness and helplessness disappear in the depth of this peace and we are at home within. Even regrets and sadness are washed away from the fabric of our being. This is the realm of the heart, of the soul, of the divine, or whatever you want to call it. The names do not matter.

I have been fortunate to know this possibility. I hope these understandings will help you to let the peace find you. The obstacles to a safe, comfortable, peaceful departure are real. They are physical, psychological, and social. We have the ability to move over or around these obstacles. Just as we prepare for a good birth, we can prepare to be free of suffering at our departure. This is our real potential. The efforts are simple, though not necessarily easy, but let's just see them clearly.

Recently the wife of a friend sent me a text message to let me know he had finally died. Her husband had a long fight with recurrent cancer. He tended to be angry and even bitter about his difficulties with the misery of chemotherapy and the inefficiency of doctors and hospitals. During his last days in the hospital, however, things changed.

She wrote this: *The little drop that carries Mark's soul merged last night with the ocean of love. I feel eternally grateful to have witnessed his transition from suffering to peace and to the beyond.*

This transition happens slowly if we have the eyes, the ears, and the heart to see, hear, and feel this reality of the life force leaving; then the pain of loss is softened forever. We become carriers of these moments; we can call them the golden threads of our humanity.

My hope is that the goodness of palliative care, medical care, and finally social hospice become more obvious as time passes. We could emulate the Greeks who had two schools of medicine: one to diagnose and treat disease, and the other to tend to the needs of the dying — to help them be comfortable, pain free, safe from harm, free of regrets and at peace. Why not have this as a simple goal for all?

Stand Still.
Stand very, very still
so the peace can find you.
— Prem Rawat

33. The food of outer life and the water of inner life

IN THE EARLY DAYS OF MY MEDICAL CAREER, I TRAVeled back and forth from the U.S. to India to practice medicine and learn from that culture. In those years, I came to understand that there are two distinct, complementary purposes in life. One is to create a wonderful outer life and the other is to discover and cultivate a rich inner life.

We each need different things for our outer life. Like food, it will depend upon the menus of our families, cultures, and eventually our own choices. We may desire wealth, friends, family, a home, perhaps a car or boat, travel, or a retirement community on a golf course. The billions spent on advertising and social media fuel our imaginations for all the stuff we can buy and all the costumes of status we can wear. They pump up our fears that we will never have or be enough.

In contrast, the need for a rich inner life is like water. It is the same for each of us simply because the source of inner contentment is already contained in our being.

As mentioned at the beginning of the book, I had learned something of this truth after seeing an inspiring kind of contentment in the people of the small remote villages in Lesotho, Southern Africa, where I lived as a volunteer in my third year of college. I had grown up in a wealthy suburb of New York City, and the lack of running water, plumbing, electricity, beds, showers, and baths in Lesotho's villages was both a shock and a liberation. The joy of life and peace that I saw in those people was transforming for me and my sense of purpose.

After my first two years at Dartmouth and then my half-year in Lesotho as a volunteer in the flying doctor service, I continued college at Columbia University in New York. This was my introduction to the distinction between achievement and fulfillment. As a premed student at Columbia College in New York, I majored in Asian studies. The literature and philosophy of India, China, and Japan spoke of this need for a rich inner life to balance the challenges of getting and losing, success and failure, and indeed, life and death.

If we can accept that we too shall die, then perhaps we can prepare, at least internally. It is never too late to come home to the peace that exists in the life force. Actually, if we have the luck to reach advanced old age more or less intact, we are generally free of a lot of distractions and then the peace of the life force can become more obvious. It was there with us all along, but a busy life can make it harder to appreciate. The best news is that we can resolve regrets, express love, forgive ourselves and others, and enjoy the beauty of existence, right until the end. This makes for a truly elegant last chapter.

Life is never made unbearable by circumstances,
but only by a lack of meaning and purpose.
— Viktor Frankl

34. Becoming young

This story is included with the permission of Betty Young

A PSYCHOLOGIST FRIEND REACHED OUT TO ASK IF I would be willing to take care of a patient who was a well-known, elderly actor. For many years she had treated this patient for depression and alcoholism in the same California town where I had my general practice. Now this celebrity was living at home with a new challenge: Alzheimer's disease. There was a staff of caregivers, but the family was looking for a doctor to visit regularly and oversee the staff and the medical treatments. The house was a five-minute drive from my office and I trusted my friend's judgment, and so I agreed.

Only then was I told the name of my new patient, and I was astonished to learn that I'd be treating Robert Young — the most renowned TV doctor of my generation. If you've ever seen *Father Knows Best* or *Marcus Welby, MD*, you're familiar with the exemplary characters Robert Young portrayed. Marcus Welby was a cultural icon, the standard for kindness, goodness, and wisdom in the practice of medicine. People used to say, "Well, he's a good doctor, but he's no Marcus Welby." I was rocked to my core to hear of the actor's personal struggles, which had included stays at mental hospitals and a failed suicide attempt.

None of the turmoil he had experienced was visible when we met. I was greeted at the door by the most senior caretaker, really the home manager who reported directly to Robert's daughter who held medical and legal power of attorney. She took me into his bedroom where Robert was sitting at the edge of his bed, surprisingly elegant in his striped pajamas. While frail and thin, he was still an extremely handsome man, and he received me with a firm handshake and a warm smile. His eyes were bright and animated, and I was struck by his gentle, engaging manner.

Even during that first brief meeting, Robert's kindness and generosity shone through. As the home manager introduced me to Robert as his new doctor, she sat beside him on the bed. She mentioned that she used to watch *Father Knows Best* religiously as a girl and loved how Robert called his daughter "Princess" on the show. "My father was a truck driver," she confided to Robert, "and he never called me Princess."

As if on cue, Robert looked directly at her and said, "Princess, you look beautiful today." She melted.

Robert then turned to me and said that he didn't think it was a good idea to play his old TV character in that way.

"What do you mean?" I asked.

Here he was, he said, widely known as this great father, but in fact he suffered serious problems with alcoholism and depression.

And even though he had been very public about his struggles, people still confused fiction with reality.

I knew what he meant. The idealism of his TV show had affected me as a child; I had wished that my father was more like the great Robert Young. Like Robert, my father suffered from alcoholism and terrible depression. He died suddenly of a heart attack before I'd had the chance to process the pain and suffering he'd unintentionally caused his family. To know that the TV father I'd grown up idolizing and yearning for also had feet of clay helped me to let go of some of my judgment of my father. I could only imagine how it must have weighed on Robert to play the revered father on TV while knowing how flawed he was in real life, making him feel like a fraud and a failure. My heart went out to him.

Robert then told me about an incident from his Marcus Welby, MD days when he'd unsuccessfully lobbied the show's director to change some of his dialog with a patient, and he asked for my professional medical opinion. When I honestly agreed that the revision Robert had suggested was a more realistic option, he was clearly pleased, and I felt our bond growing deeper. It was as though I now was not only his new doctor, but his trusted professional colleague. I was charmed. That was the first and last time Robert spoke of his celebrity past. From that point on, over the course of several years, we were always in the present together.

Visiting Robert in his comfortable, well-maintained home was a welcome break from my busy practice. The house, though modest in size, was open and full of light, with a secluded garden and views of the nearby hills: a lovely place to rest and heal from the stressful life of celebrity. I would stop by every couple of weeks to see how he was doing, chat with him and his caregivers, and make sure that the right staff was there and doing right by him. Robert was a confident man with an aura of success about him, yet he lacked a big ego and it always felt good to be around him, no matter what was going on. I suspect that his personal problems had humbled him.

Robert's decline from Alzheimer's was a gradual one: a steady diminishment of speech and memory. A sensitive man, he struggled at the outset with bouts of anxiety and agitation (both of which can accompany advancing Alzheimer's), as well as lingering depression. Yet despite all of this he was at ease with himself and I wanted to support that feeling and let nothing get in its way.

Some of the staff had goals for Robert that had nothing to do with his choices. It was as though they were trying to create a picture-perfect tableau of a celebrity at ease in his old age. They would rouse Robert from bed to have breakfast and read in his garden, even as Robert fought fiercely to lie in bed for as long as he wanted. It was dismaying how adamant these experienced and well-meaning caregivers were in trying to force him to behave in a manner they considered productive. Productive for whom?

There would even be battles over Robert's daily bathing routine. Robert had a shower that was custom-built for him yet — for whatever his reasons were — Robert hated that shower. Still, his caregivers quite literally fought with him, to try to get him into it. It was a long time before I was able to convince them that giving Robert a simple sponge bath while in bed was sufficient. He enjoyed that.

I worked with each caregiver until they could adopt an attitude of kindness and acceptance, allowing Robert to be exactly as he wished. His needs were obvious. If they couldn't get with the program, they were dismissed. We had zero tolerance for unkindness, no matter how well-meaning and experienced a person might be. I witnessed a different downside to celebrity when one caregiver we fired went to *The National Enquirer* with a fabricated story about how Robert was being neglected by a pack of thieves stealing his money and possessions: it was a wild accusation that the newspaper published without any research. For a few days after that, reporters circled the house like vultures. We avoided them, knowing that whatever we said would only fuel their scandalmongering.

A key principle of a good departure is to allow a person to do it their way and without fear. Robert was going to die slowly, because Alzheimer's disease is slow. He had heart disease, but that wasn't a problem. For over three years we managed to find caregivers who would simply let him be. And as Robert was embraced with the kindness and love of the staff and allowed to rest and do what he wanted, his suffering started to evaporate. Giving him this time, space, and care was a very rare gift without compromises — an ideal chapter which unfolded at his own pace.

During the many months of overseeing Robert's treatment, I witnessed this good and self-aware man unwind from a lifetime of achievement — and the tension between his iconic public persona and the demons he wrestled with privately — and return to a state where he was experiencing the joy of simply being alive. Far from being reductive, the process enlarged his spirit in a way that was inspiring to witness and a testament to the innate healing power and wisdom of the human being.

One fine spring day when I went to see Robert, he happened to wake up. I asked him how he was. A beatific smile crossed his face as he emanated peace.

"Perfect," he said in the sweetest way.

I could see that he was indeed feeling perfect, and then I saw his critical mind switch on as if he were thinking, "You can't say that." I told him it was okay to feel perfect. He smiled at me and went back into his blissful state.

Toward the end, Robert slept peacefully for three or four days at a time like a well-tended infant, accepting only water and a little soft food. Then he would wake up suddenly and be transformed into an adult again. He'd eat ravenously, watch TV, and request that friends be invited to come visit. He'd play the gracious host, and a great time would be had by all. Later, he'd confess that he didn't remember any of them. "Good actor, eh?"

There came a night when I was paged because Robert had no blood pressure. Anticipating that this was the end, his caregivers were already gathered around the phone when I arrived, talking with Robert's daughter and lawyer. Yet to me, Robert looked just as he did when he was sleeping. I cupped his hand in my own and put my fingers on his pulse; his heart was still beating. Could he really be dying? I continued to sit quietly with his hand in mine, feeling his pulse. And then, just like that, his pulse stopped. His heart had stopped. Doctors are not trained for this moment, and for a wild instant I even worried that I had caused Robert's death.

One of the caregivers held a mirror under Robert's nose to confirm there was no respiration—just as the first breath is the sign of life when an infant is born, the last breath clearly signals the end. There was no condensation on the mirror. Good exit, smooth as silk. No belabored breathing, no gasping or gurgling, no suffering.

The curtain had come down on Robert's last act, and he could not have staged it better. With the life force as producer and director (and us as the supporting cast), Robert had played the best father, the best doctor—and the best death. It was a remarkable performance. We stood back and applauded spontaneously.

The next day, I got my 15 minutes of fame when the news media reached out to me. It felt good to be able to tell the plain, unembellished truth: Robert Young died peacefully, of natural causes. Such a simple, even clichéd, statement. Yet it spoke to the transformation of a lifetime.

This was the best of social hospice before I knew what to call it.

It takes a long time
to become young.
— Picasso

35. Dementia need not darken departure

THERE IS GREAT FEAR THAT THE RISING TIDE OF COGnitive decline, dementia, and Alzheimer's disease in the United States will prevent anything like a safe, comfortable, peaceful departure. I have seen the very real pain and suffering that both parties feel when someone is departing with problems of memory, orientation, a loss of their decision-making ability and poor coordination. The stress reactions of fighting, fleeing, and freezing as a result of the frustration and fears from these losses always makes thing worse. Acceptance and understanding make things easier, although sometime these qualities are hard to find, especially if everyone is tired because of a lack of help.

The frustration of a person struggling with cognitive losses can be exacerbated by the frustration of relatives or even excellent caretakers. This creates volatile situations and can lead to the not-infrequent problems of elder abuse. Infants and small children need understanding and kindness rather than orders to behave the way we want them to. So too do the competent and successful adults need understanding and kindness as they become day by day like children once more.

I know from experience that some cultures consider the decline of cognitive functioning in the elderly as normal. In fact, in some cultures advanced old age is considered a time to know what we knew as children. There is a joy in just being alive and that life is about exploring, not achieving. In India when you see a happy old person, you call them Baba, and when you see a happy infant you call them baba. Same, Same. In villages when an old person with dementia is wandering about, who do you think cares for them? The police, nursing home staff, the firemen? No, it is the children that lead them home for lunch or dinner.

Once a man,
twice a boy.
— A COMMON PROVERB

36. Reverend Peters: Do beliefs help?

REVEREND PETERS HAD ADVANCED HEART DISEASE. A friend of his family, who happened to be one of my patients, asked me to see him at home. This friend was afraid that Mrs. Peters was becoming seriously exhausted and in danger of becoming sick herself. She was the lone caregiver to her large and very ill husband.

I visited their elegant, old-fashioned home where each room was kept with care and love. That is, except for the bedroom with a hospital bed that contained a semi-comatose man. That room was dark and very sad. His wife was exhausted and overwhelmed, not only with his illness but also with all that she needed to do for him. She was a sweet, gentle person, clearly at the end of her rope. As I talked with her, it became clear that she was stuck being his principal caregiver because they had no children, no close relatives in the area, and not much money.

I suggested we admit him to the hospital. He had very good cardiologists during the many years of his chronic heart disease.

I knew there would not be anything we could do to reverse his heart disease, but at least it would give her a break. She was most grateful for this intervention. We admitted Rev. Peters to the hospital. My friend Dr. Harris Kenner, a cardiologist, confirmed that there was nothing we could do to revive his heart and concurred that it would be kind to keep him in the hospital for some days and let his wife rest. This type of respite care might be called palliative care these days. It was something we could do in the 1970s when insurance companies did not reign as supreme as they do now.

Once in the hospital, Rev. Peters continued in his semi-comatose existence — unable to speak to me or his wife, but I began to hear his story from his loyal wife. He was a highly respected clergyman man in the Washington, DC area, who devoted his life to the church and was so inspiring that presidents came to hear him. He liked to write poetry about God. She was very proud of him and had tried not to be disappointed that they never had any children.

When the sun goes down, the hospital can be a different place altogether than it is by day. One of the staff on night duty told me that the Reverend would wake up at night and that they would discuss his fear of death. This young nurse assistant was helping him to not be so afraid. It seemed helpful, so I told this to his wife.

"That's impossible!" she declared, clearly aggravated. "He has helped hundreds of people die trusting God, how could he be afraid?"

In hindsight, telling the Reverend's wife of his fear of death was not such a good idea. She'd sacrificed a lot of her life for his cause, including not having any children. She avoided me after that, but I still talked to the nursing assistant and heard about his nighttime conversations and coaching. He felt that the Reverend was afraid to die because he had not done everything in his life just right.

Perhaps it was the nighttime conversations or just the relief of not being at home that allowed him to die peacefully over the next couple of weeks. He had been sick and miserable at home for months. I never spoke with him and I don't think his wife was able to before he died.

A month passed; his wife came to see me to apologize for her anger toward me. She knew I was trying to help her understand the long agony of his last months. Her understanding had shifted, and she saw that he had every right to be afraid. Just because he was a clergyman didn't mean he couldn't also be afraid.

I told her of my remorse in giving her the idea that it was his fear that kept him hanging on so long. She explained that she had hidden behind his cloak of what she called "righteousness," a cloak that shielded her from doubt and fear. If her husband wasn't afraid, all was well. She realized that she could not rely on anyone, even her husband, to shield her from a process that she too would have to go through. What a bittersweet conversation that was for both of us.

■ ■ ■

Connecting to the peace of our life force and the meaning of life is an individual effort. Some think this effort is very difficult while we are alive. I think this depends upon motivation and understanding. In my experience, if a person has a keen desire, or perhaps better to say a passion, to feel a connection with the life force, it becomes for them an enjoyable process of opening and feeling. The life force, or if you prefer, the divine, is known in feeling.

I don't know what happens when you die, but besides religious beliefs, near death experiences are evidence that it's all going to be okay. According to Dr. Raymond Moody's research, people who have almost died feel that they are in the presence of this beautiful light, and there is peace. People who have these experiences don't particularly want to come back. But when they do, they are transformed for a while. They are much more impressed with the beauty of life and are not so caught up with desires and worries. They all have this strong desire to pay attention to two things: enjoying life and learning to love. Remember Mr. V and his over twenty near death experiences. He had no particular religious beliefs, but he had no fear of death. Beliefs can lead to experience and that is good, but beliefs without experience may not be enough to reduce the visceral fear of dying.

As a physician, I trust the most what I can observe and understand practically. I like the approach of William James, father of American psychology, in his classic work, *The Varieties of Religious Experience*. James' interest in religion was to determine not whether personal religious beliefs are true, but rather how these beliefs affect a person psychologically. In his book, he describes religion as a platform that contains a holy book, a place of worship, and some sort of priesthood of people who know more about the holy book than others because of their studies and devotion. Being on the platform will affect people differently. Some benefit and some do not. Overall, James expressed that to know the divine or what I call the life force is possible without religion. To be honest, this is my preference, too. The next two stories have to do with what I perceive to be the difference between belief and experience when it comes to resolving one of the fears some of us have about dying.

Anything can make me stop,
look and wonder,
and sometimes learn.
— Kurt Vonnegut

37. Silvia: An inspiring near death experience

SILVIA WAS QUITE ANIMATED AND MENTALLY SHARP, a sweet-tempered person living in an old, fading body. Although never in physical pain, she was physically diminished and without the inner resources to make physical efforts. The old saying "use it or lose it" was true of her — no fault, just wearing out. She lived in an upscale, comfortable nursing home with a pleasant and attentive staff. Whenever I would visit, I coordinated with her son so we would be there at the same time. Despite her pleasant environment and lack of physical pain or even a progressive disease, at these meetings she always asked to die.

I did not like to hear her pleas for death; having her son there gave both of us some moral support in dealing with her seemingly irrational appeals. We didn't understand her pleas.

Silvia had lots of choices for food and activities — not such a bad life compared with other possibilities. She still looked good with her pert gray hair, beautiful face, and mostly relaxed manner.

She was not suicidal and had no intention of taking her own life. The staff reported that she was generally cheerful and responsive during the day and comfortable by night. In the presence of her son, I would give my response to her plea: "You don't have to eat or drink and you will die naturally of dehydration and starvation over some days or weeks. You might feel uncomfortable for a few days but then you will be okay and perhaps become euphoric. We will not put in IV fluids or a feeding tube. It is your choice and no hard feelings."

She would decline and carry on her life until the next visit. I began to think that her life held no meaning for her. She was not sick or in pain, but what was her purpose? What did her life mean at this point?

Reading Atul Gawande's brilliant book, *Being Mortal,* sparked memories of this woman. Dr. Gawande attributes the institutionalized lack of meaning as the cause of much suffering in the nursing home population in the United States.

Today there are many creative endeavors being made to give nursing home residents purposeful activities. One initiative is to have residents cook a large meal together in the facility's big kitchen and then serve the food to people at a homeless shelter. Another lovely idea is to create reasons for the elders to engage with youngsters at nearby preschools. There are many creative ways for very elderly and disabled people to have individual and communal meaning in their daily environment.

One afternoon I got a call from the hospital. Silvia was in the ER with rectal bleeding. I arrived, and as usual her devoted son was there as well. She was semi-comatose and quite anemic.

Clearly rectal bleeding in a woman of her age was a potentially deadly event.

Not wanting her to die in the ER, I arranged for Silvia to have a blood transfusion. It wouldn't solve the underlying problem of the bleed, but it would give her some additional time. In those days, we didn't have MRIs or CAT scans, so detecting the source of the bleed was difficult without surgery—and she was not a good candidate for surgery. She would almost certainly die with anesthesia and the first cut.

Today, aggressive ER doctors and specialists would get a CAT scan and possibly consider surgery for a tumor if a patient got better with blood transfusions and fluids. But technical knowledge without human wisdom can be dangerous and costly. So called "futile medical care" can suck up 10 to 15 percent of Medicare costs in the last few months of life. Dr. Jessica Nutik Zitter's book, *Extreme Measures: Finding a Better Path to the End of Life*, chronicles this issue. She was an ICU doctor doing futile medicine until she saw the harm she was doing by applying technology without wisdom. She writes with clarity and hopefulness from the traumatic trenches of futile care.

We admitted Silvia to the hospital. She got her transfusion and over the next few days she was better than ever. In fact, the reprieve from death had a subtle but profound effect on her. She stopped pleading to die. Perhaps the near-death experience gave her the inspiration to enjoy her existence for as long as she still had the blessing of breathing. Perhaps just this existential awareness can make life beautiful even without much external meaning. Consider the Nazi concentration camp prisoners that Viktor Frankl describes, feeling inspiration from within themselves in spite of the horrendous insanity of the camps. Like a small seed deep in a rocky crevice reaching for light and water, a seed in us seeks life no matter what.

A few weeks later, Silvia was back in the ER with pneumonia. She was comatose and there was not much hope for effective treatment. The son and I conferred, reflected individually, and agreed that this was a good time to let her go. We would have had to do a surgical procedure to get into a vein to give her antibiotics and fluids. Even then she was already so far gone that it would be futile care. A consultant might want to throw her into the ICU. We admitted her to the hospital and she was in a room with no treatment for a day before she died. The nurses, aides and ancillary hospital staff remembered Silvia from her admission. They had liked her from that time and this time they came to visit her during the day and night before she died because there was a palpable peace in her that they appreciated. It was a sweet time for all of us. Perhaps her brush with death had shifted something in her. Maybe discovering a final sense of inner peace became a purpose for her after such a long time of living without a purpose.

38. Brenda: What you cannot lose—your immortal self

BRENDA TRAVELED FROM ENGLAND TO CALIFORNIA with a very advanced lung cancer. She came proactively to fulfill a few bucket list items. She was quite sick physically but a powerhouse mentally and emotionally. She had a very full, active life of high achievement and complex relationships. Now in her sixties, she radiated a certain emotional toughness and joy of life. Her friends in California asked me to be her medical home-base and hospice coach.

A red Corvette was her car of choice for living in California, and she insisted I drive it as fast as I wanted when we went from my office to the local deli for a large, very high calorie lunch. Her time was spent in and out of the local hospital as the cancer grew stronger. In between hospital visits for her failing body, she was able to attend her daughter's wedding and a friend's wedding in Las Vegas. Her attitude was golden. She would fight the cancer with all her might while also preparing to exit gracefully.

This is indeed the effective and real two-handed approach to a serious life-threatening illness. On the one hand you are fighting and bucking to beat the disease, and on the other you are preparing to depart peacefully and gracefully if the disease wins. With these two hands, one can be the conductor of this magnificent last symphony, using both hands to keep all the musicians together, moving forward, in a beautiful tempo. One hand is there to enlist the best medical care, change bad habits, and live fully in the shadow of the disease. The other is to find those core qualities of self-contentment and kindness, and live there.

Brenda's initial course of highly toxic chemotherapy in the UK had not stopped the tumor growth. Fortunately, she had few side effects with that treatment, so she was not afraid to try a new experimental immunotherapy. This therapy was unsuccessful and made her quite ill.

Everyone who understood her predicament appreciated that she was seemingly sailing on smooth, inner-life waters. She was resilient and not afraid to assert her needs. The spread of this terrible cancer caused some awful physical problems for her, but her calm state of mind remained surprisingly intact until very early one morning when she phoned me. She apologized for the pre-sunrise wakeup call. It was the first time she had called me for an emergency—her specialty doctors were quite competent and responsive to her needs.

She'd had nighttime terrors but had decided in the darkness to wait until the light of the day to call me to see if she felt better. Her night had been a storm of utter darkness, full of emotional agony—a raid on her inner well-being. The light of day did not resolve the inner darkness. Why now, why so deep, why so dark, why so overwhelming?

After a lengthy conversation, a revelation emerged. She had suddenly realized that very soon she would lose all contact with the cherished people, places, and things of her life. The penny of departure had dropped into place. Such an uncompromising reality brought her to her knees. The pain, frustration, and fear were more real than any positive attitudes, wishful thoughts, or blind trust.

As I accepted her dark, dark state, she relaxed a little. We could step back from her panic and reflect. She had known from the initial diagnosis that she would die from this cancer. Her calm was a result of her acceptance combined with the hope of living fully in the shadow of the cancer. She was doing that very well, so it perplexed her to suddenly face a fearful mortal reality. Her agony of losing everything reminded me of a story from the Upanishads that I had read long ago at Columbia College as part of my major in Asian studies. The Upanishads is an early classic of Indian literature, a much loved text on the nature of human existence by Indian sages.

The story goes that a young boy was in agony after his father, a great sage, suddenly died. The boy, Naciketas, was quite young, and somehow his anguished crying affected Brahma, the god of creation. Brahma called Yama, the lord of death, and asked him to soothe the child because Brahma was sad to hear his cries. Yama went to the boy and promised him wealth, prestige, marriage, and children so that he would be hopeful and not cry. He told Naciketas that his father could not return from the realm of death. Yama left, feeling he had accomplished his task. The boy continued to cry.

Brahma again summoned Yama and insisted that Yama return and make things okay for Naciketas. Yama offered the boy even more riches and worldly delights — he would become an emperor with many wives and children and great power and wealth.

His further promise of fantastic success and riches had no effect on the boy. Curious, Yama asked Naciketas why all these wonderful gifts were not good enough for him. The boy replied that all these things belong to Yama and someday he would take them back, just as he took back his father. Yama was stunned by his wise insight and asked him what he wanted. The boy replied that his father had talked of an immortal self that is never destroyed and is an eternal source of love, joy, and peace. He wanted to know that. Yama fled quickly and Brahma, hearing this request, was pleased. In the next scene, Naciketas is at the feet of a master who could teach him to know his immortal self.

This story transformed me when I first read it over sixty years ago, and now it felt risky but appropriate to share it with Brenda. We talked about all that she would soon be losing and we also talked about the something that she cannot lose. If she is not aware of the immortal self then, yes, it is all loss and darkness.

The Upanishads story returned Brenda to her calm, hopeful self with a slightly new orientation. In the days that followed, she was able to finish her bucket list, resolve a few regrets, and return to her seaside home in England without any more nights of terror.

Because I could not stop for Death —
He kindly stopped for me —
The Carriage held but just Ourselves —
And Immortality.

— Emily Dickinson

39. Anna: Be with the god within you

ANNA WAS NOT A NUN, BUT SHE CHOSE TO DEVOTE herself to the Catholic faith. She was the unmarried, chaste Irish housekeeper for a very important Catholic clergy members in New York City. Her role was considered almost more devout than that of a nun, though she didn't have any special status or clothing. She had lived a quiet life of service for over 50 years and was a great source of pride for her family.

Anna's niece Maria was a nurse and a patient in my practice. She asked me if I would be willing to accept her aunt as a patient if she came to live in Bethesda with her. Maria explained that her aunt had a serious cancer and was unable to fulfill her responsibility as a housekeeper. It was complicated because Anna's New York doctor was telling her that she had a chronic lung infection when she actually had an aggressive lung cancer. The doctor had confided the true information to Maria because he felt that Anna was too emotionally vulnerable to handle the diagnosis of cancer.

As a nurse though, Maria felt that her aunt needed to be accurately informed of her real diagnosis so that she could fight the cancer. Moving to Bethesda would allow Anna to have a chance to be in a clinical trial at the National Institute of Health. Maria told me that Anna had always lived in the protected environment of the households of senior clergy in New York City.

This was back in the mid-1970s when such a paternal attitude was not unusual among older doctors. Maria and I were of another generation and agreed that Anna should know the real diagnosis so she could fight the cancer with the medical resources available to her in Bethesda. I accepted to be her doctor and Maria arranged to speak with Anna's doctor in New York. The doctor seemed quite experienced and kind. His opinion was that Anna was emotionally immature and sheltered. He did not think she would be able to deal with the scary diagnosis of cancer. Listening to him, I found myself thinking with the arrogance of youth that he was merely a paternalistic older doctor sheltering her from the possibility of getting better with treatment somewhere else. This judgment on my part would be a mistake that caused all of us to suffer.

When I first saw my new cancer patient, she came in on her own two feet. She didn't look terribly sick. She was a serious person, overweight, and very self-contained. Her big, thick glasses made her seem fuzzy and distant. I asked her what she thought was wrong with her. She explained that her doctor had said she had pneumonia, but she thought it was cancer. So, Maria and I were encouraged: Anna knew she has cancer, good. Out of respect for the New York doctor, I asked her what she would do if she did have cancer.

"Oh, I'd just ask the good Lord to take me without any pain or problems."

That seemed hopeful, but as I discovered, her hopefulness was naive, like a child's wishful thinking. Unfortunately, I was acting on the concept that she should know so we could fight it. I told her that she indeed had cancer. Perhaps there was a possibility of curing this cancer, or at least putting it into remission. I explained all this to her, but she did not hear anything. The New York doctor was right.

Her descent into unconsciousness literally happened in a so called New York minute. We admitted her to the hospital where she quickly regressed mentally and emotionally, becoming like an unhappy withdrawn child. Perhaps she had asked the good Lord to take her and he did not. She wouldn't cooperate with our attempts at diagnosis or treatment, nor did she attempt to communicate with her loving nieces. She lay in bed, mumbling and incoherent. It wasn't because she had cancer in her brain, she didn't. She was in a total psychological freeze — a primitive reaction to fear. She was not in any physical pain, but the situation was painful for all of us.

After a few days, we had to transfer her to a nursing home because she was unable to cooperate with any diagnostic studies so we were unable to find any agreeable treatments for her cancer. Once situated in her new surroundings, she just lay there. She would take fluids, but she wouldn't eat. We couldn't help.

Anna's nieces were disappointed that she did not rise to the occasion and fight the disease. The anticipation of her living in that nursing home in this kind of stupor and dying slowly without peace was distressing. I felt the pain of my ignorance.

In grappling to find something that would make a difference to her, I asked her nieces to contact the priest she had been taking care of in New York. Perhaps he could come and help her understand something. He was more than a priest—a Bishop or Cardinal in the church. He agreed to visit and came down to Bethesda. It is a day's journey back and forth. I arranged my schedule to meet him at the nursing home.

When I arrived at our agreed time and emerged from the elevator on Anna's floor, the priest was ready to enter the elevator and leave to go back to New York. So, we talked outside the elevator. I was surprised that he was leaving without talking to me. I was desperate for him to reason with Anna and help her become conscious and make efforts to get better. Surely I thought, he would have some insight as to how we could mobilize her will to live or at least help her to leave in peace. Her stupor was not comfortable. As we talked, he kept looking at the elevators. He had no interest in talking with me.

I had hoped to engage his care and understanding of his former housekeeper to help us improve her quality of life. He was completely puzzled by my thinking and told me that he had just given her the last rites.

Absurdly, he came all the way from New York City to do that. A local priest could have done that when she was actively dying. I was as guilty as Anna in my wishful thinking. I had been hoping with no knowledge that her priest would work with her to improve her mental and emotional life in the face of this terminal cancer. She had taken care of him for years and now she was suffering and could potentially lie there for weeks or even months. But her priest just looked at me like I was annoying him, and then he left.

I sat down with Anna. I felt responsible. The doctor in New York was right, she wasn't ready to face her situation. We should have just kept telling her she had pneumonia, and maybe she would have been okay for a while. Denial is not a dirty word if it can prevent a person from being overwhelmed by bad news. Initially, it allows one to carry on when facing an overwhelmingly fearful situation. The naked truth is neither wise nor kind.

Of course, not ever knowing that she had cancer meant that Anna could not make conscious decisions as to whether to treat the cancer or not. Her response to knowing she had cancer was to retreat into unconsciousness.

I know this from experience, all I could do was to try my best to rectify the harm done. There was no way we could go back and change it, but in the present there was one effort I could make. I talked to her passionately about the divinity of existence and the ability we have to feel peace and love within our own hearts. I know this as experience, not belief. I was pleading with her to open up to something other than her wishful thinking.

I wanted her to make an effort to understand her potential to evolve her religious life and find some God-given inner peace in her heart. This was my effort to help her move from her stupor to something better—to feel alive. I felt she was listening, despite appearing unconscious. So, I continued to speak about her potential as a human being, separate from being a religious person. I was attempting to appeal to the self within her that had probably chosen a religious life in aspiration to be closer to the experience of God.

It worked. She woke up and looked at me with shock and gratitude. Gratitude for understanding a simple truth is expressed well in this poem by Hafiz, a great Sufi master, translated by Daniel Ladinsky:

Every child has known God.
Not the God of names,
not the God of don't,
not the God who ever does anything weird,
but the God who only knows four words
and keeps repeating them,
"Come dance with me."
"Come dance."

"Please, be with that God dancing within you," is what I was trying to communicate. She did appear to understand, and for the first time I could see some joy in her eyes and in her shy smile. I left feeling some hope for a change in her frozen state. Even a small lit candle can remove some darkness in a room and a human heart.

That night she developed a high fever. We weren't going to treat whatever caused the fever because she was already so close to the end. So, the fever stayed for a few days, and she died. Her nieces were grateful that she didn't linger for weeks or months in some kind of semi-comatose state.

40. The jewel of hope

IT HAS TAKEN ME MANY YEARS TO UNDERSTAND THE nature of hope. We need hope in facing serious illness and dying. But hope, as I have learned, is a many-faceted jewel.

Dr. Alexandra Levine taught the students at University of Southern California Medical School an important understanding of hope. She was a specialist in blood cancers. She taught that when someone is diagnosed with a severe cancer, there are three degrees of hope. The first hope is that you beat it, no matter what the odds are against you. If you're not beating it, the second hope is that you can live successfully in the shadow of the cancer. The third hope is that when it is time to go, you can leave peacefully. In many ways, this third form of hope is acceptance. In essence, her message to us was this: There is always hope; it just changes form. Dr. Levine went on from USC to become the medical director of the City of Hope, a renowned cancer treatment and research facility.

To explore hope further, I read the oncologist Jerome Groopman who dissects it in his wonderful book, *The Anatomy of Hope.*

He distinguishes hope from both wishful thinking and positive thinking. The reality of hope allows us to rest and find some clarity of action. The necessity to always be positive can feel like a prison. No negative thoughts, even if they are realistic. Positive, positive, positive. I have had patients who refused to re-evaluate their treatment program for a serious cancer because they did not want to be less than positive about the cancer getting better. On the other side wishful thinking is just that. It is superficial. Asking for help blindly can abdicate personal responsibility for finding, accepting, and understanding the right kind of help. Deep, heartfelt prayer is wonderful in that the response of the heart is to feel kindness, calmness, and hope.

Real hope from the heart is powerful. In *The Theory of Everything,* a film about the life of physicist Stephen Hawking, he is asked what he held onto when his life became very dark with the incurable degenerative disease that he'd had since he was 21 years old. The question was posed to him at an elite scientific conference in his honor. The participants knew of his famous lack of belief in a Creator. His response was that there is a vast place of hope within his being and that — within that hope — there was always an action step to be embraced.

Toward the end of my practice in Bethesda, I offered seminars together with a nurse who had worked with Dr. Elisabeth Kübler-Ross, teaching nursing home nurses how to deal with dying patients. The author of *On Death and Dying*, Kübler-Ross was a pioneering doctor who had taken death out of the closet of silence. To the shock and dismay of her medical colleagues, she openly discussed death with patients and their families, a bit like

Doctor Ruth talking frankly about sex on the radio in New York City. Her classic description of the five stages in facing death holds true today: first denial, then anger, then bargaining, then sadness or depression and, finally, peaceful acceptance.

I attended an event with Dr. Kübler-Ross at the National Cathedral in Washington, DC. At that time, she was absorbed in her experience with dying patients perceiving different subjective realities as they passed away.

After her talk, the Bishop of the cathedral, who was supposed to simply thank Dr. Kübler-Ross, instead took issue with her experiences of people finding peace in their transition from this finite world to something less finite. His reaction was painful to most of the doctors and nurses present. Instead of embracing the various visions, dreams, and emotional experiences that had helped

Dr. Kübler-Ross's patients reach a good place, he asserted dogma, challenging the notion that a person could find profound peace at the wall of death without being a baptized Christian. The difference between belief and experience was never so vivid in this harsh, critical, narrow vision of beliefs, life, and death. It was sad. She shared these mostly wonderful experiences with a sense of awe, wonder, and passion, noting the curious lack of any fear, just as I had experienced with a handful of my patients.

In doing research for this book, Sushila found that the Swiss-born Kübler-Ross — while only in her twenties and against her family's wishes — traveled behind the Iron Curtain in 1946, shortly after the end of WWII. In Warsaw, she found devastation in the abandoned concentration camps, and inside children's barracks, she found thousands upon thousands of butterflies etched and scratched on the walls. How did they come to be there? Many of the children knew they would die. It became clear to her that the butterflies were a symbol of hope, etched with whatever might have been available — fingernails, pebbles, sticks. Perhaps they felt a collective hope that death was not an annihilation but a transformation, just like the emergence of a butterfly from its chrysalis. Or perhaps they simply delighted in seeing the freedom of the butterflies, to fly over the walls that imprisoned them.

The morning after learning about the butterfly etchings, Sushila ventured out to take a ride on her bicycle and was surprised and delighted to discover a beautiful jade-green and gold monarch chrysalis had formed under the seat of the bicycle. For two weeks, she did not ride her bike and cordoned it off in her yard so her children would not disturb it.

One morning, she awoke early and thought of the butterfly but decided to stay in bed rather than go to see whether it was emerging. A couple of hours later, her husband came in to say that the chrysalis was empty and the butterfly was gone. He drew the curtains and brushed something at his neck—the butterfly had landed on his neck and accompanied him into the bedroom where the children were waking. It flew to the curtain, and Sushila was able to hold it. The butterfly turned around on her finger to look directly at her and the children. They removed the screen from the window and held the butterfly outside, giving it time to ready itself. Only when it knew it was ready did it fly way.

Epilogue

THERE IS A NEW RAY OF HOPE FOR THOSE OF US WHO are very stuck in our misery, especially those suffering from early childhood or trans-generational trauma. There is a psychedelic platform of treatment for PTSD and depression. There are good studies of using psilocybin, MDMA, ketamine, and LSD to relieve the extreme mental and emotional obstacles to a comfortable, safe, and peaceful departure. I have had some personal experience with patients using these resources to heal the pain, fear, and frustration of living in a traumatized nervous system. Unwinding from a lifetime of severe stress is possible. The thirst and passion for peace is part of our being human.

It is never too late to reconnect to the life force, to the heart of peace and clarity. We absolutely do leave everything behind, but if we can feel peace, then this is our final legacy. Leaving in gratitude and peace is a whole lot better than anger, bitterness, and pain being dumped on your relatives, friends, and caretakers. Leaving in peace is a successful departure.

In a sentence, every physical body has a shelf life, a use-by date; we are perishable. But in everybody is something that does not die and can be enjoyed until and perhaps through the very end. The possibility is to become familiar with that kind, gentle, peaceful, generous nature of existence.

In being with a person who is departing slowly, we have the chance to observe the subtle change in focus from what is fading away to what is and what will be. This can be surprisingly inspiring. People wonder about hospice professionals — why do they want to be with dying people? Isn't that morbid or strange? Just like caring for a newborn, it is necessary to care for people in their last days, and that transition can be beautiful. In some cultures, death is celebrated as a great freedom. If we can see a person becoming free of suffering and feel the peace in real time, then it is all worth the effort.

Whatever our circumstances, whatever our environment,
we need to find a way to let our inner nature fully express itself.
No opportunity to do that should be ignored or abandoned,
no opportunity should be put off until tomorrow.
Even when the ground around us seems fallow,
there's an incredible world within that's full of fertile potential.
If we can start to get the light of clarity and the water
of understanding into our life, our desert will bloom.

—Prem Rawat

For Further Reading

Mitch Albom, *Tuesdays with Morrie* (Broadway Books, 2007)

Tim Bauerschmidt & Ramie Liddle, *Driving Miss Norma* (Harper Collins, 2017)

Ira Byock, *Dying Well: Peace and Possibilities at the End of Life* (Riverhead Books, 1998) Viktor Frankl, *Man's Search for Meaning (1946)*

Atul Gawande, *Being Mortal* (Profile Books Ltd., 2014)

Jerome Groopman, *The Anatomy of Hope* (Random House, 2003)

William James, *The Varieties of Religious Experience*, (Longmans, Green & Co.,1902)

Michael Kearney, *A Place of Healing: Working with Nature and Soul at the End The Healing* (Spring Journal, 2009)

Eric Kendal, *In Search of Memory: The Emergence of a New Science of the Mind* (W. W. Norton & Company, 2007).

David Kessler, *The Needs of the Dying* (Harper Perennial, 2007) Bessel van der Kolk, MD, The Body Keeps the Score (Viking, 2014)

Elisabeth Kübler-Ross, *On Death and Dying*, (Scribners, 1969)

Hadley Vlahos R.N., *The In-Between: Unforgettable Encounters During Life's Final Moments* (Ballantine Books, 2023)

Francis Weller, *The Wild Edge of Sorrow* (North Atlantic Books, 2015)

Teresa Wolf, *Hope in Our Final Season* (Maticus, LLC., 2016)

Jessica Nutik Zitter, *Extreme Measures: Finding a Better Path to the End of Life* (Avery, 2017)

Films and Videos

Alive Inside: A Story of Music and Memory (2014)

Me, Earl and the Dying Girl (2015)

Captain Fantastic (2016)

Departures (2008)

Compassion and the True Meaning of Empathy, https://www.ted.com/talks/joan_halifax

The Good Wolf and the Bad Wolf, https://youtu.be/vzKryaN44ss

Books for Children

Leo Buscaglia, PhD, *The Fall of Freddie Leaf* (Slack Incorporated, 1982)

Joyce C Mills, Ph.D., *Gentle Willow* (Magination Press, 2003)

Lynn Plourde, *Thank you Grandpa* (Dutton Juvenile, 2003)

Judith Voorst, *The Tenth Good Thing about Barney* (Prentice Hall, 1987)

Alan Zweibel, *Our Tree Named Steve* (Puffin Books, 2007)

Acknowledgments

From John Horton

To my Stella who has given me the patience, support, and love I needed for the long gestation of this book.

To the prodigy of existential intelligence, Prem Rawat, who keeps teaching me that it is never too late to discover the peace of existence.

Mary Jane Horton, my sister, for her encouragement as an early reader and proofreader.

Tim Gallwey for the Inner Game wisdom, his friendship, and encouragement.

Teresa Wolf and the other creators of Our Community House of Home, a wonderful social model hospice house. Bill Lamar, M.D. who taught me about medical Hospice. Micheal Kearny for teaching me about Ausculpian medicine, the key to a peaceful departure.

Rick Benzel, Susan Shankin, and Darcy Hughes of New Insights Press who helped create this book and get it ready for publication.

To my many friends who enjoyed listening to these stories and encouraged me, especially Sascha and Lauren Schneider, Mark Wolf, Owen Plant, Lothar Delgado, Carole Wilson, Susan Stiffleman, Joel Karchmer, Janet Goldberg, Tim Hagel, Phil and Carol Gold, Bowie Hahn, Ondine Norman, and Tammy Meyers.

Henry Reif and Wendy Lewis for their impeccable attention to detail. Mitch Ditkoff for his excellent help as a writing coach. Beth Gerber for her help in writing stories. Julie Yinling, author of Final Conversations for her early advice and support in writing this book. Chris Cannan, an early collaborator and writer for this project.

Sushila Wood for her wonderful, open-hearted intelligence and care in the writing process. Always ready for the next iteration of content, she never complained and, in spite of her family and work obligations, made time to talk. It was in these talks that the content took shape to become what we have here in this book. Truly a labor of love for both of us.

From Sushila Wood

To my husband Michael Wood, for somehow giving me space to continue to become myself, and holding it all together despite having a serious stroke. Living through stroke recovery while writing this book made it all real; I am not afraid, I know I will be okay when you or I do finally go.

To my three children, Amiya, Evelyn and Byron, you help me to see the golden threads of life. To my parents, sister and grandmothers, for giving me space to remain strong headed and find my way.

To Debbie Cations, Joy and Rolf Koren, Monika Winslow, Aine McAteer and everyone who encourages me and stands in their own power to live and express their truest heartfelt selves.

To the WISC mentors, for seeing in me beyond what I could see. To my A Lotte Horses family and especially Lotte Swauger for respecting my desire to write while also growing our riding programs; to the horses, standing in your sphere has forever changed me.

Special thanks to Prem Rawat and Tim Gallwey for bringing amazing wisdom and tools and sharing them generously.

Most importantly, to John, for seeing the value in our partnership, and always keeping it real, wise, playful, and truly delightful. You trusted in me with your life's work, yet gave me space to contribute to it with my own humble learnings. It has been a gift to walk this journey, to listen to you tell these stories again and again. Each time I hear you tell a story, I delight in learning something new.

About the Authors

IN THE TRADITION OF PASSING ON ONE'S WISDOM, these stories of mostly good departures were shared in conversation between Dr. John Horton and Sushila Wood. This co-written book is the result of their many conversations about death, dying, and facing the humble and often beautiful realities of aging.

John Horton

Born January 29, 1943, in New York City, he spent his childhood in Harrison, New York. John was a running back on a championship high school football and second in the state for pole vaulting for three years. After two years at Dartmouth College, he volunteered in a flying doctor service in Basutoland, Southern Africa. That half year was spent mostly in remote mountain villages reached only on foot, horse, or one-engine aircraft. Here he experienced village life in the heart of Africa as well as the horrors of Apartheid in neighboring South Africa. A chance meeting with Malcolm X in

Cairo on the way back to college in the summer of 1965 confirmed the simplicity and kindness in the heart of Africa.

College continued at Columbia in New York City. Majoring in Asian humanities as a premed student, he caught the eye of the Duke Medical School recruiters and Duke accepted John even though he did not have top grades or research interests. He was the senior class president and the commencement speaker. Next was a year of internship in medicine, pediatrics, and psychiatry at San Francisco General Hospital from 1970 to 1971. The counter-cultural and political upheavals of those years affected all, and lower staff levels made for a difficult year. Postponing a psychiatry residency to recover from the internship year, the now Dr. Horton started a medical clinic in India for western visitors as well as working in the student health services back at Columbia College during trips home from India.

In 1974, he began to manage the largest general practice in Bethesda Maryland. For five years Dr. Horton enjoyed a thriving office and hospital practice and taught at George Washington University School of Medicine. The next 12 years were a sabbatical from medical practice to focus on non-profit educational work in the United States, Europe, and Asia-Pacific.

For the last 25 years Dr. Horton partnered with Edd Hanzelik, MD to create a primary care/integrative medical practice in Westlake Village, California. Together they co-wrote the *Inner Game of Stress* with the well-known creator of the Inner Game Coaching model, Tim Gallwey. John was asked by Dr. William Lamers, a founder of the hospice movement in England, to co-direct an outpatient hospice in the San Fernando Valley. He was a founding board member of the Community House of Hope, a social model hospice home in Thousand Oaks.

Lecturing on stress resolution and personal wisdom has been a passion for Dr. Horton for decades. Many seminars were offered at their practice in Westlake by the doctors and for larger audiences locally with Tim Gallwey. John also worked with Tim Gallwey in Prague and Singapore.

Sushila Wood

Sushila came to see Dr. Horton first as a patient. They often discussed stress, and several years later, Sushila interviewed John for a film, and thus began their dialogue about death and dying. Out John's stories tumbled. Augmented by their discussions, this book was born.

Sushila grew up in Australia and started producing local audiovisual events and adventure travel events as a teen. In her twenties, she traveled across North America, Europe, and Asia, producing events and visual content about peace, while obtaining her bachelor's degree in multimedia and marketing. In the years since, she has produced live events, articles, and documentary content for distribution across several cultures. Sushila also now witnesses the congruence between the beginning and the end of life daily, as she supports her husband's recovery from stroke and spinal injury, while raising their three children.

Sushila is a certified Waldorf education teacher, and lives among the avocados and lemons in Santa Paula, California. In 2019, she co-founded a Waldorf-inspired equine education program for children at a local horse ranch, A Lotte Horses. She delights in designing outside-the-box community education programs to help develop a fascination for lifelong learning. She writes often about the congruence between childhood and the last chapters of life.

Stay Connected!

Please review this book on Amazon, Goodreads,
or wherever good books are sold!

To receive updates or learn more, connect with us here:

Dr John Horton
drjohnhorton.com

Facebook: DrJohnHorton

Sushila Wood
sushilawood.com

About this Book and Series

THIS BOOK IS PART OF A WRITING SERIES OF SEVERAL books called *The Heart of Medicine*. The series is part memoir, part commentary on my years as a doctor and on the human aspects of medicine. This side of medicine requires an understanding of the profoundly necessary qualities of the heart for wellbeing, happiness, healing, and the value of the doctor (practitioner) relationship.

In the heart of our being are the simple abilities we have to feel love, peace, joy, appreciation, serenity, and gratitude. These are the evolutionary gifts of being human. The intellectual capabilities that we have to understand the biology of the body and the technological abilities we have to impact this biology are the wonders of modern medicine. Understanding the heart of medicine is not an intellectual endeavor, though; it has to do with feeling, intuition, clarity, and connection.

Connection to the self is common to all of us. To be seen, to be known, to be loved, to be cared for — these are necessary for the heart of medicine to be real. It is easy to say the right words in an advertisement for compassionate health care, but for this to be real, there must be learning from the heart. It is time for the subjective realities of life to be as respected as the objective realities of science. As human beings, we need purpose and meaning grounded in the wonder and beauty of being. Seeing the charming innocence of a child, we feel alive. In our thoughts and imaginations, we can lose the feeling, the wonder, the joy of life. This is not a trivial loss, and this series aims to recapture it for you.

www.ingramcontent.com/pod-product-compliance
Ingram Content Group UK Ltd.
Pitfield, Milton Keynes, MK11 3LW, UK
UKHW041636190726
13854UKWH00006B/2531